THE CYO IN INDIANAPOLIS & CENTRAL INDIANA

THE CYO IN INDIANAPOLIS & CENTRAL INDIANA

JULIE YOUNG

THE History PRESS

Published by The History Press
Charleston, SC 29403
www.historypress.net

First published 2011

Manufactured in the United States

ISBN 978.1.60949.206.9

Library of Congress Cataloging-in-Publication Data

Young, Julie.
The CYO in Indianapolis & Central Indiana / Julie Young.
p. cm.
Includes bibliographical references (p.).
ISBN 978-1-60949-206-9
1. Catholic Youth Organization (Indianapolis, Ind.)--History. 2. Church work with youth--Indiana--Indianapolis Region--History. 3. Church work with youth--Catholic Church--History. 4. Indianapolis (Ind.)--Church history. I. Title.
BX810.C45Y68 2011
259'.2308828277252--dc23
2011023105

To every member of the CYO program…past, present and future.

Contents

Acknowledgements 9
Introduction 11

Chapter 1: Deliver Us from Evil 15
Chapter 2: Sheil's Solution 21
Chapter 3: CYO Comes to Indy 29
Chapter 4: Guide Us in Fair Play 44
Chapter 5: "Put Me In, Coach!" 63
Chapter 6: One Time at CYO Camp 75
Chapter 7: To Amuse the Mind and Arouse the Spirit 94
Chapter 8: Growing, Leading and Serving 115
Chapter 9: Senior CYO 124

Conclusion: The Future of CYO 139
Appendix: Indianapolis CYO Timeline 143
Bibliography 153
About the Author 157

Acknowledgements

From the moment I announced that my next book would be on the history of the Catholic Youth Organization (CYO) in the Archdiocese of Indianapolis, the support I received was overwhelming. I want to thank my publisher, The History Press; my commissioning editor, Joe Gartrell; my readers; and my friends who saw the potential in this project and were solidly behind me right from the start. I always appreciate knowing that there is someone in my corner.

I have to offer my deep gratitude to the good people at the CYO office who generously opened their archives to me and were willing to share their thoughts, photos and memories for this book. Having that level of support for this project made the whole process nearly effortless. Jerry and Ed, I couldn't have done this without you, and I hope that my work will help tell the CYO story in a way that will resonate with many.

I can't say enough about the number of people who responded to e-mails, Facebook blasts and phone calls and who were willing to share their thoughts for this volume. Whether it was summers at CYO camp, participation in athletic programs or entries in any number of science fairs, Hobby Shows and bake-offs, your memories have been invaluable to this project, and I would be remiss if I didn't recognize those contributions.

To Jan O'Brien, I can't say enough about your enthusiasm and willingness to share your memories and photos of your camp experiences at "the Ranch" and Christina. I hope I have done justice to your thoughts. Thank you so much for your responses to my endless e-mails and your willingness to help.

To Diane Sharp, Terry Williams, Mike Archer, Jody Davis, Greg Bierck, Kim Morey Tester, my musical soul sister Vicki Hendley, Terry Wilgus, Steve Warren, Father Bob Gilday and everyone else who reached out and made this title possible, thank you.

To the members of Eastside Senior CYO group who allowed me to crash their reunion at Fort Benjamin Harrison and who shared so many wonderful memories to include in the book, thank you. Thanks especially to Pat Murphy, Ed Trumpey, Jack Mears and Loretta Miller for providing narrative and photos. You are the best!

To Steve Barnett, your editing skills are worth their weight in gold. I could never have done this without you!

Of course, no book would be complete without my profound gratitude to the men in my life who had to put up with several months of insanity while I tried to pull together yet another book—my "Wonder Twins," Chris and Vincent. I love you more than life itself, and I am proud that you both have had the chance to be part of the CYO program in your own unique ways. You activate my every thought, you are in my every prayer and I couldn't do it without you. Love, J.

Introduction

My first experience with the CYO came when I was in the fourth grade—I had entered a homemade pie in my parish Hobby Show. I confess, my hobby wasn't really baking, but *Little House on the Prairie* was one of the most popular television shows, and I fancied myself a regular Laura Ingalls. I remember cutting the apples and rolling out the pie crust, under the watchful eye of my mother, all the while imagining that I was my favorite pioneer girl baking a pie for Almanzo Wilder.

When the baking was finished, and my pie stood on the counter waiting for the next day's competition, my parents went out for dinner and hired a neighbor girl to stay with me for the evening. A veteran of the CYO Hobby Show, she suggested that we create a presentation display for my pie, and together we found a piece of cardboard that we decorated with a smattering of autumn leaves. If I live to be 100, I won't forget the sight of this high school senior standing beneath my parents' maple tree while I pointed out the exact vibrantly colored leaves to gather. She even volunteered to recopy my recipe, to which I readily agreed. Her twelfth-grade penmanship looked much neater than my nine-year-old script.

The following day, I dropped off my pie at the school cafeteria and then went home to wait out the long day of judging. At that time, the competition was stiff. Both the cafeteria and the gym were filled with displays in fine arts, skilled crafts, kit crafts, baking, sewing and the ever popular collections. I can still see Danny and Billy Babcock's impressive display of Cincinnati Reds memorabilia towering above my best friend Jack's coin collection. Needless to say, they were perennial favorites. It took a long time for the judging to take place, and by the time we returned for the awards ceremony, it was early in the evening.

I still remember the moment I walked into the room and saw my pie, a strip of fabric glinting bright blue alongside of it. Could it be? Sure enough, lying next to my creation (with one thin slice removed from it) was a blue ribbon emblazoned with the CYO logo and the words "First Place." One of the Hobby Show coordinators told me that the judge said that my pie was the best she'd ever tasted. Today, that statement remains my biggest culinary compliment. After placing on the parish level, I was going to the citywide competition to compete against other kids from all over Indianapolis.

Though I didn't place at the city show held at the former Latin School (and home to the CYO offices), it was an experience that gave a kid like me a lot of confidence and instilled in me the quest for excellence. Cheerleading and kickball followed at a time when you had to try out for your place on the team—and not everyone was guaranteed a spot—yet I persevered, though there were moments of disappointment as well as elation. I spent four years competing at the CYO music festival, and there was also my seventh-grade air pressure project that led me to the citywide science fair at the CYO Center. Again, I didn't win, but I met so many great people, and I always had a good time!

The Catholic Youth Organization was initially a program meant to keep kids on the straight and narrow and get them off the streets of Chicago, but it has become a thriving entity that provides kids with positive role models and the chance to participate in a wide variety of programming that meets the spiritual, social, athletic and cultural needs of young people. Not only that, it also enables Catholic and non-Catholic children to be an integral part of the community and form bonds that span generations. Countless young people have benefited from CYO programs in their parishes or on a national level, and the impact of the organization cannot be overstated.

Legendary crooner Frank Sinatra said that participation in CYO activities gave kids the chance to grow into thinking adult Americans who will help build better communities and better cities. "Regardless of race, creed, or color, any boy or girl…is welcome at all times to take part in CYO programs and activities," he wrote in a newspaper editorial. The singer realized that it was important for young people to have a place where they could go and express themselves in a healthy atmosphere and know that there are people who are interested in their thoughts and ideas. "CYO attempts to give youth that feeling of importance," he noted.

Throughout the country, many have recognized the positive impact that CYO has had in their lives, whether it was an athletic league or another program that attracted them to the organization in the first place. Renee Price Fox of Ocean Pines, Maryland, said that she would not be the adult she is today without the CYO athletic program at her childhood parish in Wilmington, Delaware. After playing softball and basketball and running track, she eventually began coaching, as well, when her daughters played on a Pennsylvania CYO league. "I learned many lessons: camaraderie, team effort, respectful competition, working hard toward a goal, not to mention the friendship of former teammates and, of course, the fun, and now the memories. All of these qualities prepared me to raise a family, be involved in my community and maintain my faith," she said.

Susanna C. Bellafante-Cloud of St. Petersburg, Florida, remembered being crowned the CYO Harvest Ball Queen from her local parish, Christ Our King, in 1960. She was nominated for the title through her parish and won the crown by raising the most funds at a youth rally. "I don't recall how much money Christ Our King raised, but as the representative of the winning parish, I received a complimentary photo of my one-day reign, a beautiful bouquet of a dozen red roses and a silver charm commemorating the event, which I still have today."

Locally, CYO gave young people the chance to participate in healthy competition, show off their skills and meet like-minded people, resulting in lifelong friendships. Pat Murphy said that she met her husband through her senior CYO group on the eastside of Indianapolis, and due to her shyness, she felt that CYO gave her the best opportunity to meet other young Catholics, which helped to bring her out of her shell. "It gave me the push I needed to get out into the world," she said. "I got to know people I went to high school with on a whole different level. It was a wonderful thing."

Researching this volume was a little like playing detective. I had a couple of clues but relied on oral narratives to unlock other avenues that could be explored in order to give the CYO some historical context and perspective. I found that exploring the CYO gave me insight into the Catholic culture of twentieth-century America, and as I uncovered each new idea, I plowed into heavier research to find out more about the psychology of sports, the impact of Title IX, dating in the 1950s and '60s and other subtle nuances; all of this made this book as much a social commentary as a historical record that moves beyond Central Indiana and into a worldwide organization that gave youth a place not only in their parishes but in the larger community as well.

Whether you remember CYO "movie night" in the parish basement or were one of the many athletes who participated in one of the largest

THE CIRCLE OF CYO YOUTH SERVICE

Certificate of Achievement

This Certifies That

Julie Johnson

In Recognition of Excellence in the

1981 Cadet Hobby Show

has been Granted this Certificate, for

Baking - Class B

Given at the CYO Awards Presentation *this* 29th *day of* October *19* 81

William F. Kuntz
C Y O EXECUTIVE DIRECTOR

The author's certificate from the CYO Hobby Show for her Cadet B baking entry. *Author's private collection.*

youth sports programs on the planet or were a Hobby Show/music festival/science fair person, such as myself, or attended camp at Rancho Framasa or Camp Christina, this book is a celebration of the memories that we all share. CYO has been and continues to be the very heart of a young person's life in the church. Working with the CYO office and gleaning recollections from numerous people throughout the area, I have tried to capture the ongoing history of the CYO, whose prime, according to Executive Director Ed Tinder, "is tomorrow."

CHAPTER 1
DELIVER US FROM EVIL

Run, jump, make noise, but do not sin.
—St. John Bosco

The struggle with juvenile delinquency is as old as time itself. Beginning with the passage telling the story of Cain killing his brother Abel, the Bible is full of other stories to suggest that some kids, no matter how they were raised, were simply bad seeds—and there was little anyone could do about it. Over the centuries, parents have fought to try and give their kids a better life and to ensure that they remain reverent and obedient. In 1300 BC, a Hebrew woman by the name of Jochebed feared for her own son's safety and literally sent him "up the river" in the hopes that her beloved Moses would have a better life than the one she could give him on the "wrong side of the tracks."

Several generations later, a young Jewish mother was at odds with her preteen son when he decided to hang out in a temple for three days while the rest of his family headed for home. After hearing her son's cheeky excuse regarding his whereabouts, Mary must have wondered what she would have to do to keep her child in line, and though Luke never mentions the resulting punishment, one can bet that Jesus wasn't allowed to leave the house for the next three weeks.

Keeping young people on the straight and narrow hasn't always been easy. The issue of juvenile delinquency has been blamed on everything from socioeconomic factors to divorce rates, blighted neighborhoods, television, a lack of religion and many other things. However, in 1962, Reverend John

D. Allenmang said that these don't tell the whole story, "[f]or out of these conditions come good, normal people."

All it takes is someone willing to mentor those on the edge, those who need to find value in their lives. It takes someone willing to build character through kindness.

ST. JOHN BOSCO

The inspiring man who became the patron saint for the Catholic Youth Organization was St. John Bosco of Italy. Bosco was born on August 16, 1815, in Piedmont, Italy, in a small cabin to a poor couple who already had two other sons. It was a time of dire circumstances and great famine in the region, and by the time Bosco was two years old, his father had died, leaving his mother to care for her three growing boys on her own.

It was a less-than-ideal setting for any family, and while Margaret Bosco struggled to make ends meet, her economic difficulties prevented her from

St. John Bosco of Turin, Italy, is the patron saint of the Catholic Youth Organization. *Author's private collection.*

providing her boys with a formal education. As they headed off into the fields each day to work as shepherds, she must have wondered how her sons would ever grow into proud, strong men.

Bosco was blessed with a gift of ready wit, a good memory and a thirst for knowledge. When he was nine, the youngster experienced a series of dreams in which he realized that he was called to lead others through kindness and gentleness, rather than using strength and might in order to influence them. He also felt a call to the religious life, a dream that seemed impossible, as the priesthood was largely reserved for men of means or privilege.

Fed up with his work in the fields, Bosco chose to leave home at the age of twelve, reasoning that his departure would mean one less mouth for his mother to feed. He lived in the streets and found work where he could (usually in a vineyard), but wages were scarce, and he resorted to begging in order to get by.

Father Joseph Calosso, who noticed the boy's tenacity and intellect, took him in and offered Bosco his first formal education. In 1835, he was finally able to join the seminary at Chieries and was ordained a priest six years later on the eve of Trinity Sunday by Archbishop Franzoni in Turin.

After his ordination, Bosco moved to Turin, where he took on his priestly duties with plenty of zeal. He visited prisons with another priest, and he saw past all of the poor characteristics of the inmates (many of whom would be hanged on the gallows) and wondered what evil had influenced them so that they saw no other way out for themselves. There were children in these places who, like him, had to live on the streets and succumb to desperate measures simply to survive from one day to the next. These children were at the mercy of terrible influences in the prison system, and he knew that it was only a matter of time before they became men with only the death penalty ahead of them.

He knew firsthand how a random act of kindness could make a difference in someone's life, and he was determined to pay forward Father Calosso's gesture in a way that could be the difference between life and a life of crime for these outcasts, who were basically good people who hungered for a connection. His resolve was confirmed when he was preparing for Mass in December 1841 and a sacristan chased a young ragamuffin from the church who had refused to serve at the service.

Bosco heard the cries of Bartolomeo Garelli and reached out to him, developing a friendship and the beginnings of what was to become Bosco's first oratory, a school based in prayer that instructed children of the street and gave them the chance that society had refused them. By February 1842, there were 20 at-risk boys in the oratory, with 10 more following in March; by a year later, the number had grown exponentially, with 400 enrolled. All of them were opened to Bosco's kind and gentle manner and felt that he understood them in a way that no one ever had before.

Bosco's Mission

With numerous students, holding classes in the street was no longer feasible for Bosco, so he needed to look for a suitable location where meetings could be held. Sometimes the boys of the oratory were transient and would take long walks on Sundays, but finally he got the approval of the archbishop to use two adjoining rooms for formal study. The oratory became so popular that applications arrived from a number of surrounding areas, forcing Bosco to hold night classes for boys who worked in factories during daytime hours.

Bosco believed in recreation and fun, securing musical instruments for his pupils and encouraging them to have fun and be free. Not everyone was enthusiastic about his work, and it wasn't long before he had to abandon his little rooms and deal with obstacles that threatened to ruin his efforts with young people entirely. There were naysayers who wondered about the mental stability of a man who ministered to "undesirables," and they were so persistent that they threatened to have him committed to an asylum. Over time, the oratory was moved from its first home in Rifugio to St. Martins, onto St. Peter's Churchyard and eventually to a few rooms in Via Cottonlengo.

With seven hundred boys enrolled in the school, Bosco lived nearby with his mother, who had left the family home, and all that she had, and dedicated the last few years of her life to her son and his work. She lovingly responded to the children, who referred to her as "Mama Margaret," and had no issue with selling her belongings in order to meet the expense of room and board for these young men in the first Salesian (named for St. Francis de Sales) home.

In time, others began to recognize the work that Bosco was doing and saw it as an important ministry, one that should be preserved and continued. Municipal authorities helped him secure funding for technical schools and vocational workshops. At one point, Bosco was even able to build a church in the Valdocco quarter of Turin. It was an ambitious undertaking that was met with many setbacks along the way, but finally, with the help of some generous friends who supplied Bosco with about $200,000, the church was consecrated on June 9, 1868.

Many have tried to explain why Bosco's oratory was so successful, but its success was attributed to Bosco's method of mentoring young people and being willing to push past all of the surface "dirt" in order to capture the spirit within. Bosco's method of study did not rely on any form of punishment, and he instilled in his students a sense of duty in order to achieve their obedience. He also strove to appreciate his students, offering them a sense of self-worth. "I have always obtained, and from apparently hopeless children, not alone what duty exacted, but what my wish simply expressed," he wrote in 1887, according to the *Catholic Encyclopedia*.

By the time Bosco died in January 1888, his work had grown, and there were 250 houses of the Salesian Society throughout the world, which ministered to 130,000. Out of this group, Bosco had selected the brightest among them and furthered their education with instruction in Italian, Latin, French and mathematics. More than 6,000 priests emerged from the institutions, and 1,200 continued the mission of the society.

The St. John Bosco medal is the highest honor the CYO can bestow on someone for his or her commitment to the youth of the area and the organization that serves them. This is the first group of honorees from the Central Indiana area to receive the medal. *Courtesy of the Indianapolis CYO.*

Bosco's method to educate and mentor young people was so successful that many adopted the system to use on those who might otherwise not be given a chance in society due to their social or economic backgrounds, not to mention the troubles they might have already encountered. However, when Bosco was canonized in 1934, no one could have imagined his impact on a new program developing in a Windy City half a world away.

CHAPTER 2
SHEIL'S SOLUTION

There are no problem children… We are the ones who have failed.
—Bernard J. Sheil

The Roaring Twenties was a time of loose living and great excess that dominated the American landscape in the third decade of the twentieth century. Conformity and conservatism were out, and a modern, metropolitan lifestyle was in. Women bobbed their hair, shortened their skirts and took part in a sexual liberation unknown to prior generations. Men of questionable repute often went to work for one of the organized crime bosses, serving as a rumrunner for the local speakeasy, where one could enjoy an elaborate meal, live bands, lots of liquor and plenty of "atmosphere." It was a time of urban crime, which was romanticized in dime novels and cinematic efforts such as *Public Enemy*, *Little Caesar* and *Angels with Dirty Faces*. The boom, which gave some sectors of the economy the chance for prosperity that they may not have otherwise enjoyed, came to a sudden end with the stock market crash of 1929.

By 1930, about one-fifth of all inmates in the United States prison system were teenage boys coming from poor neighborhoods who had been enamored of the "glamorous" criminal lives of noted gangsters such as Al Capone, Lucky Luciano and Hoosier native John Dillinger. The National Prohibition Association even met in Atlantic City to discuss the problem of juvenile delinquency and what communities could do to keep kids off the street and out of trouble.

Bernard J. Sheil was no stranger to the "lost boys" of his own city of Chicago. He was raised in the streets at the tail end of the nineteenth century merely eight blocks, but worlds away, from the Skid Row life that these young men endured as unloved thugs-in-training with no one and nothing to turn to.

Sheil's own parents, James and Rosella, could be described as a middle-class couple who filled their home with love. Rosella was thrifty with the family funds, while James, though equally responsible, was known as a generous spirit who was often a "soft touch" whenever he heard a hard luck story. As a young man, Sheil distinguished himself as a scholar athlete who eventually attended St. Viator College in Bourbonnais, Illinois, graduating with a Bachelors of Arts degree in 1906.

His prowess on the baseball diamond made him a hot prospect for clubs such as the Chicago White Sox and the Cincinnati Reds, but he gave up his passion for sports because his calling to the priesthood was much stronger. After four more years of study, Sheil was ordained in 1910.

A HARSH REALITY

As a young priest, one of Sheil's duties was to serve as a part-time chaplain at the Cook County jail, where he accompanied more than one inmate on his "final walk" along death row. One particular man struck a chord with the young priest when he asked why people waited until the end to offer comfort and support, according to a *Time* article, "The Bishop's 25th": "Why do they wait until now before they start to care?" After witnessing one too many hangings, Sheil vowed to do something to reach these young men before it was too late.

In 1928, Sheil was named the auxiliary bishop of Chicago. He was forty years old and known as an outspoken advocate for the underprivileged and marginalized. He believed in the goodness of people and never forgot about the convicts he had met in the prison systems who were basically good people and might have lived a different life entirely if only they had positive role models to look up to when they were younger.

Sheil was determined, by 1930, to see if he could save a few souls before youngsters were too far gone that there was no pulling them back. He told Chicago cardinal George Mundelein that he wanted to develop a program that would give children productive activities in a supportive atmosphere in the hopes that it would keep them off the streets and out of the correctional system. Designed to be a boxing club, Sheil wanted laypeople to serve as partners in the program along with local priests who knew their parishioners and their problems better than anyone else.

"It's not a club for juvenile delinquents. It's a wholesome, energy-absorbing ambition firing action for every boy, and I mean every boy—the good, the bad, the indifferent…That's the only way it will work," Roger L. Treat said.

Cardinal Mundelein was intrigued by the proposal and approved the ambitious yet unconventional project, but he told Sheil that he needed to secure his own funding in order to get it off the ground. Using his inheritance from his father, in addition to a $10,000 gift from another man, Sheil set out to convert the potential youth criminals by giving them a social and athletic program that was all inclusive. The result was the Catholic Youth Organization (CYO).

The CYO Is Born

The CYO was built on the initiatives of the charitable Holy Name Societies and started with youth centers that were set up around the city to give kids a place where they could drop in after school, have a healthy forum in which they could release their ambient energies and find loving and caring people willing to listen to their thoughts and mentor them in a positive way. Religious denomination aside, the CYO welcomed all young people into the program and kept the sermons to a minimum.

According to the *Encyclopedia of Chicago*, "The CYO offered a wide ranging system of social services, community centers and vacation schools; but its greatest publicity resulted from an extensive sports program that claimed the world's largest basketball league (430 teams) and an international boxing league."

Those boxing clubs were one of the initial programs that gained momentum early in the organization, and when Bishop Sheil came under fire for the popularity of such a physical and aggressive sport, he remarked, "Show me how you can inspire boys away from the brothels and saloons with a checker tournament and I'll put on the biggest checker tournament you ever saw," according to *Time*.

Through the CYO program, Sheil impressed on his athletes that their skills in the ring could be their tickets to college and a better life for themselves. Boxers were often exposed to the "dirty side" of the business that promised fast and easy money through nefarious channels. Sheil knew that the bigger fight was the battle for the soul, often tempted by the quick and easy path. "If a boy is going to fight, it is better for him to do it under our auspices and under the watchful eye of his priestly friend and superior than the back of a speakeasy," he said, according to Treat.

Bishop Bernard J. Sheil was the catalyst for the establishment of the Catholic Youth Organization, a boxing club that began in Chicago, Illinois, in 1930. *Author's private collection.*

In June 1932, Sheil opened the CYO Center at 31 East Congress Street, which came with plenty of space for the fighters, as well as fifty-two bowling alleys. The building became the central hub for the movement, and while financing the acquisition of the building has always remained a mystery, Sheil said that God provided for the CYO through contributions.

Thousands of fighters began training at the building, but Sheil began broadening his horizons from the boxing world. His endeavors included more sporting opportunities, the School of Aeronautics, vacation schools, Boy Scout troops (under the CYO banner), a home for parolees and the CYO Band.

According to Robert L. Treat's *Bishop Sheil and the CYO*:

> *Each boy who came to the CYO was an avenue to the heart of a social problem. As Bishop Sheil moves from symptoms to cause…the Bishop's peculiar genius reveals itself. Bishop Sheil didn't invent Boy Scouts or boxing tournaments…any more than he invented colleges…he reviews the situation, makes a decision…surveys all the means at his disposal… deploys them to the best advantage and brings them to bear with a crashing force on the point he has decided to attack. This is how he built the CYO.*

Another "Machine Gun" McGurn

Among the success stories of the CYO, Ernesto "Blackie" Giovannangelo was typical of the mobster wannabes who found his way into the program and turned his life around forever. Blackie was a tough kid with even tougher acquaintances in his westside neighborhood. He could beat up any kid on the block, knew how to steal and picked up pocket money by running alcohol for a local bootlegger.

Blackie was also a target of racial profiling, unable to get a job due to his Italian heritage (thanks to the local Italian mobsters who provided an image that all Italian-Americans were up to no good), and he saw several of his friends picked up by the police simply for the way that they looked. He also remembered the bloody wreckage of the St. Valentine's Day Massacre and realized that he was living on borrowed time. How long would it be before he succumbed to the same life as the guys around him? How long until he was another Al Capone, Patsy Tardi or the late Jack "Machine Gun" McGurn?

Blackie had heard that there was a priest downtown advocating a boxing league and decided to check it out. "That was the crossroads," he said in December 1950, according to Treat. Giovannangelo became involved in the CYO program and eventually secured a job, saved his money and received a college education. He served three years in the military and ultimately became the director of the CYO's Westside Center, where not only did young boys have the chance to work out their aggressions, but mothers and other family members were welcome, too. "I could have gone down in front of a gun like Jack McGurn did in 1936. I can't help believing that God reached down and gave me a nudge when it was almost too late," reported Treat.

A Crusader for Social Justice

Sheil became one of the most beloved and well-respected Christian leaders in the country, not only for his work with children, but also for his work with the underserved and marginalized. His commitment to social justice included procuring guide dogs for the blind, offering special education classes and behavioral therapy and aiding hundreds of Puerto Rican women who were brought to the city through employment agencies to work as maids in Chicago-area homes but ended up in virtual slavery. As Treat wrote, "[They] were unable to collect their just wages, and, with no money available, unable to live any place except the most disreputable, unclean places which passed for rooming houses."

Additionally, if the young ladies *were* able to get their wages they were owed, there were language and assimilation barriers that they faced as well. Sheil heard about their plight and worked to rectify the situation by creating the Puerto Rican Program of the CYO, designed to provide social, recreational, spiritual and educational opportunities. Though it lasted a mere four years, as many as six thousand Puerto Ricans benefited from the program.

The man who spearheaded the CYO was not without controversy, however. Sheil was a well-known proponent of the labor movement and actively spoke out on issues that he felt were important, no matter what the consequences might be. That outspoken nature earned him several enemies over the years. Sheil believed strongly in organized labor and collective bargaining.

In 1939, he appeared on a Congress of Industrial Organizations (CIO) union platform in solidarity with the packinghouse workers who were on the verge of a strike. Never one to shy away from what he felt was important, he

Bishop Bernard J. Sheil during one of his famous speeches. Throughout his career, Sheil was a proponent of social justice and of helping youth reach their full potential. *Author's private collection.*

was warned that such a move could be misconstrued and might thwart any chance he had of future promotions within the church. A *Time* article quoted him as saying, "I wasn't ordained a Catholic priest in order to become an archbishop," as he approached the podium.

It was a no-holds-barred statement of support for the rights of the common laborer. He said that "the returns of [a worker's] labor must be sufficient to enable him to bring up his children properly. This includes not only the necessities of life, such as adequate food, clothes and shelter, but also necessary medical care and reasonable education. A wage which does not meet these requirements is an unjust invasion of fundamental and natural rights," according to Treat.

While his position seems reasonable, company owners, many of whom had been generous supporters of Sheil's work, were chagrined at the thought of contributing to a pension plan or paying for medical care and increasing wages for their employees. They saw the union movement as a way to let the employees dictate the terms of the working environment.

It was not the only controversy in Sheil's career. When Frances Sweeny, a Bostonian Catholic school teacher, spoke out against anti-Semitism, she was forced to give up her position. Sheil was outraged, and after her death, Sheil made sure that her voice did not stand alone. Speaking at CYO headquarters, he reminded the people gathered that Jesus himself was Jewish and was raised in a Jewish household. He also said the Jewish traditions were important and should be honored and respected. Despite his impassioned speech, a woman came forward and denounced Sheil as a bishop. "You're a Rabbi!" she screamed, spitting on his face.

Sheil remained calm. "I thank you madam for your action and your words. Rabbi? That is what they called our Lord," he responded, according to Treat.

In 1942, Sheil established the CYO Educational Department with its first project, the Sheil School of Social Studies, to "show people a picture of life as it can and of right should be." Sheil was determined to discipline young minds, enlarge their scope and offer them a social conscience, as well as give voice to the greatest of human truths.

A Lasting Legacy

Throughout the 1940s, the CYO program that Sheil began continued to grow and flourish throughout Chicago. By the time of his twenty-fifth anniversary as auxiliary bishop in 1953, the Palmer House in Chicago was packed with

2,300 supporters from all walks of life who wanted to pay tribute to Sheil and his life's achievement. His little CYO movement had grown, and with a staff of 500 to help him run the Chicago office, hundreds of additional centers had been established throughout the country.

But Sheil's ambitious programs had spread his resources too thin, and without the support of his generous benefactors (who were disheartened by his liberal stance), Chicago's Cardinal Samuel Stritch became more involved in the CYO inner workings and asked Sheil, who had several health issues, to resign his post as CYO director-general. As a result, many of the programs were cut or transferred to other charitable agencies. Sheil remained the auxiliary bishop and pastor at St. Andrews Parish in Chicago until 1966, when the Most Reverend John Patrick Cody suggested that he step aside and let someone younger take over. Sheil initially agreed with Cody but ultimately told reporters, "I didn't retire, this is a removal," according to a *Time* magazine article.

Sheil, who died on September 13, 1969, would be known as the greatest friend that the American youth ever had, and he always vowed to fight for a better world—"[a] world where poverty and destitution will be only a melancholy memory—a world where laughter and innocent joy will replace suspicion and hate…I shall never stop fighting for that kind of world," he said, according to Treat.

Thankfully, his message continued in Chicago, as well as in other areas, including Central Indiana, where the laity, the priests and a forward-thinking bishop with similar values and vision made sure that CYO would be an integral part of Hoosier children's lives.

CHAPTER 3

CYO Comes to Indy

Recreation should be wholesome and supervised.

—Bernard J. Sheil

The success and notoriety of Sheil's movement inspired dioceses all over the country to adopt CYO programs on the parish level that would help young people develop the essential elements necessary for Christian maturity. Areas such as Detroit, Milwaukee, New York, Cincinnati and San Francisco jumped on board with the program, and Indianapolis wasn't far behind. In 1938, Father August R. Fussenegger and Father Charles Schoettlekotte, who were both chaplains for the Knights of Columbus (K of C), approached Bishop Joseph E. Ritter (later Cardinal Ritter) about forming a youth organization to meet the needs of boys and girls in the Central Indiana region.

Ritter Sees the Need

Like Sheil, Joseph Ritter was passionate about social justice and sensitive to the needs of young people. Named the seventh bishop of Indianapolis on March 24, 1936 (following the death of Bishop Chartrand), Ritter was known for reducing the debt of the diocese by $3 million, reorganizing the Catholic charities in the city and desegregating the Catholic schools eleven years before the State of Indiana ended segregation in public education—and sixteen years before *Brown v. Board of Education* put an end to segregation in public

Along with members of the Knights of Columbus, Cardinal Joseph E. Ritter is responsible for bringing the CYO to Central Indiana. *Cardinal Ritter Junior and Senior High School.*

schools nationwide. His decision was met with resistance from members of the Ku Klux Klan, who protested the move with public demonstrations outside S.S. Peter and Paul Cathedral on Meridian Street in downtown Indianapolis.

Ritter was intrigued by the idea of bringing the CYO to the Circle City. He appointed Schoettlekotte as the first city director of the CYO, and by the end of the year, a number of organizational meetings had been held in order to help get the program off to a solid start. One memorable meeting took place on December 12, 1938. The K of C hall was packed that night as the membership listened to keynote speaker Jack Elder, a former Notre Dame football player and, at that time, athletic director of the Chicago CYO program. He waxed poetically about the success of the organization and shared that much of that success was due to the number of young priests who served as moderators and coaches for the various programming.

"Priests were often the coaches in those early days. Of course, that was back in the day when there were three to four priests assigned to each parish. The youngest ones were often in charge of the CYO programs or the youth programs at their parishes," said Ed Tinder, executive director of the CYO in Indianapolis. "More importantly, the establishment of the CYO helped organize programs that were already in place. It was a central body to consolidate expenses and a cost effective and logical way to get the job done."

Early organizers during the last years of the Depression were so committed to the program that they not only pledged their time and talent but also worked to raise $12,000 for the infant program. According to Edward J. Fillenwarth Sr., president of the first CYO Board of Directors, some of the early board members who went above and beyond the call of duty time and time again included American Fletcher National Bank president Frank McKinney and construction entrepreneur Francis Wilhelm.

"No one knows to this day how much these two men did for CYO without anyone knowing about it except for a few board members who by chance found out, usually long after the money and deeds were forthcoming," wrote Fillenwarth.

Tinder said that the entire Wilhelm family was a constant source of support for the CYO: "Phil Wilhelm coached, he was an athletic director, he managed the gym at Our Lady of Lourdes, he was a board member and president and he was very generous. He was a man of amazing generosity, and he had a compassionate heart. He was a pleasure to be around at all times. The Fillenwarth family was another group who offered multigenerational support of the program and made a huge difference to the Indianapolis CYO."

With a board of directors in place and seed money in the bank, the CYO began planning programs and events for young Catholics in 1939. The first official event was a citywide dance held in the auditorium of Cathedral High School on Meridian Street, with more than one thousand young people in attendance representing every parish in the city.

Before long, the first baseball leagues were coordinated and included twelve teams on the high school level and fourteen teams in the senior league. According to Fillenwarth's article in *50 Years of Golden Memories* (the CYO annual report of 1988–89), a tennis team, a dramatic competition and other activities were not far behind. "Almost from the beginning, the CYO in Indianapolis, as in Chicago, was energetically and enthusiastically supported," he said.

Janice (Beck) O'Brien became active in Sacred Heart's CYO program when she was a girl in 1957. Though the organization had been going strong for nearly twenty years at that point, she was still struck by how active a program it was that was supported by parents and clergy alike:

> *Our moderator was Father Simon, a Franciscan priest, and our meetings were in the basement of our grade school where we had a bowling alley and the CYO club rooms. Kids would come from all over the city to our CYO on Sunday evenings from 7:00 to 10:00 p.m. We would play the jukebox, dance, play cards, talk and play ping-pong. It was a great time, and a lot of my classmates would come from the surrounding south side parishes for a fun evening.*

Jody Davis, a member of St. Andrew parish, remembered how willing parents were to act as chaperones for the CYO activities or drive to various events: "They were so committed and never complained. They were just happy that there was something for us to do and something for us to be involved in that kept us active within our parishes."

THE WAR YEARS

In January 1940, Father Maurice Dugan was named the new director of the city's CYO program, but within a few months, Father Richard Langen had taken over the post and formed the Junior Youth Council to plan and round out programming and activities for the organization. There was great hope and optimism for the movement during the sleepy, peaceful and early days of the decade. That all changed, of course, on December 7, 1941, when the Japanese bombed Pearl Harbor and thrust the country into World War II.

Overnight families said goodbye to husbands, fathers, sons, uncles and brothers before banding together to buy war bonds and stamps and collect rubber and tin, not to mention ration coffee, sugar and other necessities so that everyone could have their fair share. It is a tribute to those who were left behind that the CYO continued to flourish and grow during the war years, especially when everyone in every city and town was overextended with patriotic duties. The organization also became an integral part of the war effort.

World War II–era dances were very popular for the early CYO members. This photo shows a "circle dance" during a Catholic USO event at the local K of C hall in 1943. *Courtesy of the Indianapolis CYO.*

In an effort to keep CYO members connected to the community, the *CYO Bulletin* was published and sent not only to local members but also to every CYO service member deployed overseas. No doubt those GIs were grateful for any piece of news from home. In addition, Father Langen was quick to organize Sunday afternoon and evening socials for servicemen at the local K of C hall. The National Council of Catholic Women (NCCW) and local parishes provided food and support for the gatherings, which allowed young people to dance the night away (often with a live band) and create memories to last through months and years of separation, as well as long nights on the battlefield.

"I never thought about it before, but it is amazing that the CYO did survive the war years at all," said Fillenwarth's son, Ed Jr., who was also a CYO board member until the early 1990s. "It goes to show how committed the city was to the CYO movement and how those early organizers, my father included, were committed to helping keep the program on track."

In 1943, Father Richard Kavanagh became the new CYO director for the city, a position that he maintained for the next twelve years. The following year, the diocese was upgraded to the status of an archdiocese, and during his tenure at the helm of the youth program, Kavanagh was instrumental in overseeing the CYO's assumption of the Catholic Salvage Bureau and the beginning of a CYO radio program called *Youth and Religion*, which was broadcast on WISH. Archbishop Paul C. Schulte also appointed deanery CYO directors in order to help manage the burgeoning program, which helped delegate some of the responsibilities beyond one individual.

In 1945, an exciting opportunity opened for the CYO when Bert and Julia Dingley made a gift to the organization of 280 acres in Brown County to be developed as the first CYO summer camp in the area. Named Rancho Framasa, in honor of the couple's three children, the first camping session took place in the summer of 1946.

A camp committee was formed, with Monsignor Albert Busald, pastor at St. Philip Neri, as the chairman. The camp was given a grant by the Lilly Endowment for a water filtration system, and additional money was received from Archbishop Schulte for the construction of a dam for the reservoir lake.

Mrs. Fred Haunss was largely responsible for the camp fund drive, as well as other public relations efforts that helped generate interest in the camp. Before long, there were many children begging their parents to send them to "the Ranch" for a week in the summer so that they could have an adventure in the great outdoors.

That same year, it was decided that there needed to be a centralized location for CYO sports in the city, and a committee was formed to begin

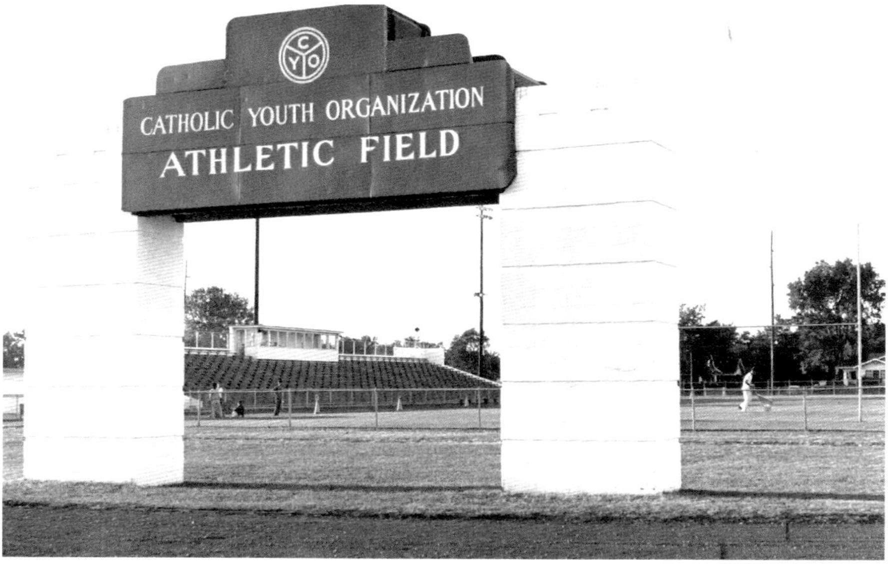

The CYO athletic field in downtown Indianapolis was a centralized sports complex for football and track events. *Courtesy of the Indianapolis CYO.*

planning the construction of a CYO stadium downtown. Harold Miller was the chairman for the stadium committee, and in 1947 a thirteen-acre property was purchased at Sixteenth and Harding Streets (across the street from Bush Stadium) that would be developed for CYO sports. Like with the camp fund drive, a second fund drive was held for the stadium project, and construction was able to start a year later. The formal dedication of the property occurred on September 12, 1949, just before a double-header football game between Cathedral and Sacred Heart High Schools. The postwar CYO era, full of possibilities, had begun.

PROMISE AND HOPE

After years of sacrifice and scarcity, the 1950s must have felt like a breath of fresh air to those who toiled tirelessly during the World War II years. GIs were home and anxious to find good paying jobs, start families and reconnect with their parishes. It's no wonder people wax nostalgic about the decade as an idealistic time in American history. The CYO was not immune to the wave. Just ten years after its inception, the CYO was riding high. The early part of the '50s saw the CYO accepted as an agency of the Community Chest (today the United Way of Central Indiana).

With camp, sports and social opportunities abounding, the CYO sought to expand its offerings by adding an Archdiocesan Youth Council, the One-Act Play Festival, a Junior Style Show, the National CYO Convention, the Catholic Quiz Contest (sponsored by the *Criterion* newspaper), a baking contest and an interparochial music fest designed to give young people with varied interests a chance to shine. "At that time, kids weren't as scheduled as they are today," said Father Bob Gilday, a CYO board member and pastor of Little Flower church on the city's eastside.

The first CYO banquet was held in 1954 to honor several benefactors with the St. John Bosco medal (CYO's highest honor) for outstanding service. The first class of inductees included Mr. Earl J. Owens, Mr. and Mrs. Fred Haunss, Mr. and Mrs. Bert Dingley, Miss Winifred Galvin, Mrs. Agnes P. O'Conner, Miss Marjorie Boyle, Mr. Edward J. Fillenwarth Sr. and Mr. Leo

The CYO banquet was an annual event that the archdiocese looked forward to as a way to honor those people who had contributed to the program, as well as the CYO chapters that had showed outstanding spirit throughout the year. *Courtesy of the Indianapolis CYO.*

Tom Joyce receives his St. John Bosco medal in 1975. *Courtesy of the Indianapolis CYO.*

Evans. The success of the program also led to the construction of a new CYO office next to the stadium with funds provided by the archbishop. On September 18, 1958, the building was formally dedicated and fully staffed.

The CYO continued to grow and flourish locally. By 1960, the enthusiasm for youth programs had reached a fever pitch. The election of the nation's first Catholic president certainly helped the excitement along. John F. Kennedy's youthful zeal and call to action encouraged young people to become involved in a number of activities. More young people than ever were involved in the CYO, both on a junior and senior level, which fostered the need for more adult advisory committees that could help the program reach even greater heights throughout the decade.

One committee was the St. John Bosco Guild, along with its Ladies Auxiliary. The ladies planned events for the CYO and served as a public relations component for the program as well, sometime before a full PR team could be identified a few years later. Thanks to her work with the Summer Camp Fund, it was no surprise that Mrs. Fred Haunss was elected

The CYO office building was constructed adjacent to the athletic field just off of West Sixteenth Street in Indianapolis. *Courtesy of the Indianapolis CYO.*

Archbishop Schulte dedicates the new CYO office building, which was used until the offices were moved to the location of the former Latin School on Stevens Street near Fountain Square and next door to Holy Rosary Parish. *Courtesy of the Indianapolis CYO.*

the first president of the group, and her contributions to the CYO have been invaluable over the years.

The Priests' Advisory Committee was made up of priests from all of the deaneries. It was designed to assist the CYO executive director in each of the five aspects of the program: spiritual, emotional, athletic, social and cultural. Members of the committee also helped with retreats at every level, attended youth meetings and were available as presenters at other meetings, as well.

Finally, the Public Relations Committee came on board in order to help the organization maintain a positive civic image and to develop good relationships with the media while identifying publicity opportunities for the CYO. The committee also assisted with the planning, implementation and promotion of the CYO's long-term efforts.

Another addition to the CYO program during the 1960s was Camp Christina, a southern Brown County property purchased with funds provided by Mr. and Mrs. William B. Anstead Jr. and used as a primitive summer camp for girls. Additional funds were secured through a $15,000 donation from the Inland Container Corporation Foundation for the construction and

The Public Relations Committee was one of the first committees formed to help the CYO grow and flourish in the early years. *Courtesy of the Indianapolis CYO.*

The St. John Bosco Guild Ladies Auxiliary in 1962. This group was instrumental in helping the CYO with fundraising efforts and public relations. *Courtesy of the Indianapolis CYO.*

installation of a water filtration system. Camp Christina's inaugural season began in the summer of 1965 with five one-week sessions.

There were also the odd improvements and expansion of CYO's various facilities throughout the decade, as well. However, an era that began with so much promise became a period of lost innocence and turmoil. The assassination of President Kennedy weighed on all Americans, and the onset of the controversial Vietnam conflict, together with the upheaval within the church following the Second Vatican Council, brought about many changes that would affect millions of lives. Young Catholics in Central Indiana saw the CYO as a port in the storm and clung harder than ever to the programs that they loved. Those programs would be a foundation of self-awareness and social responsibility for generations to come.

NEW DIRECTIONS

In the 1970s, the CYO of Central Indiana began to shift with the wave of modernization that was moving through the Church as a whole. The same wave that brought about the Mass in English encouraged the CYO to modernize while remaining connected to the mission of the early days: to mentor all children, regardless of background or religious denomination, and to provide support of those volunteers who give of their time to work with the youth of the area.

According to the 1988–89 annual report, "In 1970, the CYO Board of Directors expressed concern for providing a better community base for the organization and its activities." The Priest Advisory Committee engaged in a two-year study of the cadet (grade school) program eligibility rule and recommended to the archbishop that it was prudent to allow the non-Catholic children to participate in CYO activities. With the approval of this recommendation, the individual parishes were given the chance to include these children as part of their CYO programs, and many of them did.

William B. Sahm became the executive director of the CYO in June 1973 and was devoted to the idea of expansion and modernization of the organization. When he passed away, the post was assumed by Mr. William F. Kuntz, who became a dedicated leader of the CYO in the archdiocese.

Kuntz was a 1950 graduate of Butler University and a member of the school's football squad, on which he served as a captain in 1949. He was a high school football coach and a teacher at Scecina Memorial High School before taking on his role as executive director for the CYO. Everyone who knew "Bill" (who died in 1984) talked of his dedication to others, and service is no stranger to the Kuntz family. His son, William A. Kuntz, has also played an active part in the CYO movement, serving as a board member and coach, not to mention being a generous (and anonymous) benefactor to many. His daughter, Michele Kuntz-Wood, has been a leader in the city's annual Susan G. Komen Race for the Cure event in conjunction with her duties as a nurse and her work with other local organizations.

William F. Kuntz continued to develop the CYO program and upgrade facilities, including the move of the CYO offices from their home on Sixteenth Street to the newly renovated Latin School on Stevens Street. Kuntz also worked with the Catholic Salvage Bureau in order to help send needy kids to summer camp (an experience that many say changed their lives forever) and worked to develop youth leaders out of existing CYO programs. He also oversaw the formation of training programs for adult volunteers in hopes

A shot of a CYO dance in 1978 shows that although there were many activities changing for the organization, popular ones such as dances remained the same. *Courtesy of the Indianapolis CYO.*

of providing the best in Christian leadership for anyone involved in CYO activities. The initial training offered was called SPERO, and it was provided through a number of other workshops and seminars throughout the latter half of the 1970s. While it was believed to be an effective training method, in 1979 the CYO Leadership and Service Institute became the umbrella program to train and certify CYO volunteers.

Youth programs took on a very different look in the 1980s thanks to the youth ministry movement sweeping the nation in a number of churches and denominations. Tinder said that the youth ministry movement adopted by U.S. bishops was designed to be more comprehensive than the CYO program. During that time, parishes moved away from the CYO logo (other than athletics and specific CYO-sponsored events), and the old CYO moderator for the local parish became the "youth minister" in charge of not only youth activities but also religious education and other parochial offerings. "These youth ministers were responsible for a lot more than merely organizing drop-ins in the church basement," Tinder said. "They were now in charge of confirmation, CCD and much more comprehensive programming than they were when they were the CYO moderator."

Youth ministry programs aside, the CYO programs that had been the foundation of the program remained the cornerstone of the organization, which required the continued training and certification of additional adult volunteers. According to the 1988 report, "The administrator of Volunteer Services was responsible for the creation and implementation of the new certification program." In October 1980, the CYO held its first Leadership and Service Institute, which was designed to help people develop leadership skills and qualities in a way that would help them be effective youth leaders. The institute also helped those leaders understand the spiritual, psychological and emotional impact they had on the young people in their charge.

There was also a need in the early 1980s to create a new position known as the administrator of teen services. Duties for this position included working with high school–age youth and helping them become more involved in CYO activities while also developing the youth ministry program for the organization.

Since 1983, participation and involvement in CYO youth ministry has increased dramatically, with more high school–age youth participating than ever before. CYO retreat programs ("Quest" for freshman and sophomores; "Search" for junior and seniors, along with the "Christian Awakening Retreat" for seniors) are filled to capacity. The CYO Archdiocesan Youth Conference attracts more than eight hundred youths each year, and young people from all over the archdiocese have actively participated in pro-life activities, peace and justice workshops, Christian Leadership Institutes and the Advent Vespers Service, according to a CYO report.

"I will never forget one retreat that I attended at Camp Christina in Brown County," said a 1987 retreat participant. "We went to Mass at the amphitheater and could look out eleven miles over the horizon. It was beautiful, and then in the middle of the homily a deer walked through. I may not remember much about the readings, but I remember feeling very close to God during that service."

"Senior retreat was special for me because it gave me a chance to reflect on the different relationships I had, both good and bad," said Janine Rigg, who attended her Christian Awakening Retreat while her mother was battling terminal cancer. "It also helped me realize the strength my mother had while going through her treatments, supporting her family and serving as the primary breadwinner. I didn't have many years with her after that, and I think retreat helped open some doors for our relationship that I doubt would have been opened otherwise."

In addition, there has been no shortage of participation in the traditional CYO youth activities, such as athletics, music festivals and science fairs, which continue to bring children into a program in which they can thrive and grow.

"Our mission remains the same as all of the religious education programs in the Catholic Church: to pass on the Catholic faith, values and traditions and to teach a gospel message," said Tinder. "It may look a little different, and the number of activities is different than what they were in the 1960s or '70s, but the number of participants is significantly higher."

Tinder said that throughout the latter part of the twentieth century, and into the dawn of the twenty-first, CYO was and is constantly evolving and changing, but it is still offering young people the chance to remain connected to their parish families and to one another. From its humble beginnings as a way to keep kids on the road to righteousness, to becoming a thriving and resourceful program, the CYO has experienced many growing pains as it changed with the times. With so many more opportunities for children, some are in sports training all year long and playing in travel leagues, in addition to their CYO-level or IHSAA commitments. Others are in the Indianapolis Children's Choir or in their parish youth choir, which takes up a lot of their time. Tinder said that kids are busier today than they ever have been in years past, requiring some events to fall by the wayside, but they are well rounded and very connected to their parishes through their required service hours and personal initiative, which drives them to live their faith on a daily basis. "It just looks different because so much of those things are organized now on the parish or school level, people do not think of it as a CYO activity," he said.

Tinder also noted that the survival of the organization runs parallel to many other Catholic entities that have learned to tighten the belt and sacrifice in difficult years, but the passion and commitment of the participants, moderators, coaches and benefactors is what keeps the organization going. "It's the belief that the purpose of the organization is greater than the program that appears to be on the surface," he said. "That commitment is what we are all about."

CHAPTER 4
GUIDE US IN FAIR PLAY

It takes quick thinking…and real courage to defeat an adversary.
—Cardinal Mundelein

Athletic teams have been the very heart and soul of the CYO since its inception. Sports competitions offer young people the opportunity to learn fundamentals such as discipline, teamwork, perseverance, fair play, the thrill of victory and the agony of defeat from a Christian perspective at the grade school and high school level.

According to Steve Silverman, a writer for the Lance Armstrong Foundation's website, participation in sports is something that all children can benefit from: "It may begin with tossing a football back and forth with an older sibling or father or kicking around a soccer ball with neighbors. At some point, the youngster decides that he enjoys sports and wants to play. Organized sports can give a child a chance to have fun and grow from the experience."

While any number of youth sports organizations claim to be the oldest in the country, it is a safe bet that Little League baseball was among the first organized sports groups in the nation. Sports programs offer children the chance for healthy competition and a way to exercise self-control. I Corinthians 9:25 states, "All who take part in the games train hard. They do it to get a crown that will not last, but we do it to get a crown that will last forever."

It's a Knockout

Bishop Bernard Sheil understood that many of the young men involved in early CYO activities were full of pent-up anger and frustration. They desperately needed a healthy way to release that energy rather than taking it out to the street, where they were likely to get into trouble. The solution was boxing, a sport perfectly designed for angry young men with something to prove.

Boxing was full of controversy long before Mike Tyson or Muhammad Ali ever entered the ring. In fact, it was banned in many states due to its violent nature. When New York legalized the sport in 1920, Chicago wasn't far behind. One of the first major tournaments held in the Windy City was sponsored by the *Chicago Tribune* and eventually became known as the Golden Gloves. In 1930, Sheil and the CYO entered the ring, transforming the gym of St. Andrews into a complex for youth boxing matches. The club proved to be a popular diversion during the Depression era, according to

Bishop Sheil made boxing an integral part of the CYO program and gave young men the chance to get their aggression out in a healthy environment. *Courtesy of the Indianapolis CYO.*

the *Encyclopedia of Children and Childhood in History and Society*: "[CYO Boxing] supplied its members with a full suit of clothes as well as medical and dental care. CYO fighters who opted for the professional ranks received guidance from program affiliated management teams. Others got jobs through the Catholic social and commercial network."

The success of the boxing program became one of the highlights of Sheil's work with the CYO sports program. Many of those early boxers traveled internationally in order to represent the United States, the Golden Gloves and the CYO in the Olympics. The Chicago History Museum noted that most of the early CYO boxing athletes came from poor and underprivileged backgrounds and that this opportunity helped them become professional boxers over time.

It wasn't only boxing that Sheil had his hand in, though. He was a proponent and sponsor of basketball, speed skating, track and field, swimming, volleyball and other sports teams that gave all children a chance to compete. At one time, the CYO basketball league was the largest in the world, with more than 400 teams and ten thousand players. There were also 160 heavyweight teams, 140 lightweight teams and more than 90 girls' teams competing in the league, all before 1940, according to the Hoopedia website.

The Catholic youth sports programs have three goals: to empower young people to live as disciples of Jesus Christ in our world today; to draw young people to responsible participation in the life, mission and work of the Catholic faith community; and to foster the total personal and spiritual growth of each young person.

"PLAY BALL!"

When the CYO came to Indianapolis, the various sports leagues already in existence at the parish level were merged and came under the direction of the CYO banner. The organization was able to streamline teams into a singular unit, where there would be plenty of opportunity for young athletes, both on the elementary and high school level. According to CYO executive director Ed Tinder, the decision offered expansion possibilities and economic advantages for future years: "I wasn't involved in those early days, but can you imagine the expense if each parish had to hire its own athletic director to schedule games, not to mention its officials?"

The purpose of the CYO athletic program in Indianapolis, according to the handbook, was to provide supervised competition for boys and girls at their own age and ability levels so that they could feel their personal worth within a team forum. It also provided a competitive spirit in the proper perspective that fostered personal skills improvement and promoted a sense of pride, responsibility and accomplishment to participants and the adults who served as coaches and moderators. Athletics was geared to provide youths with the experience of success and failure at an early age and to expose the youth to a greater perspective of church and society through broad-based scheduling, not to mention a training and recreational activity that fostered physical development, according to the CYO handbook.

"It's hard for people to draw that bridge between a gospel message and a football game, but I tell coaches that when they are on that field they are in the laboratory. This is the real-life experience," Tinder said. "As athletes, they learn to conduct themselves and act as Christians on the field. They will see coaches get frustrated, and sometimes they will make the wrong decisions, and through competition we learn just as much as we do in a classroom."

An early shot of the Little Flower CYO football team coached by Father Pfau, Father Richard Kavanagh, Mr. Lee Evans and Ed McLaughlin. Football was one of the first CYO sports that allowed private parochial teams to be part of a league. *Courtesy of the Indianapolis CYO.*

A football action shot taken at the CYO athletic field. Those who played on the field called it the nicest in the city and a superior facility compared to public parks. *Courtesy of the Indianapolis CYO.*

The first CYO football championship was between St. Catherine and Little Flower and occurred on November 12, 1939. Nearly ten thousand spectators descended on Christian Park to watch two undefeated teams battle it out in the Super Bowl of CYO matchups. St. Catherine had proved its prowess, having already won three championships, but this game, for the CYO championship, made a victory slightly more profound, and the players were going up against a fierce competitor.

Little Flower's offense, honed by Father Richard Kavanagh and Lee Evans, along with powerhouse players such as Joe Touhy and Fred Queisser, was more than enough of a match for St. Catherine's, and the team took home the inaugural title with a final score of 14–6, giving the eastside parish the first CYO championship football team, according to Little Flower's fiftieth anniversary book.

The variety of sports offered at any given parish was dependent on the level of interest, availability of equipment and practice space, not to mention having a priest or other responsible adult capable of coaching the team. In those days, there were a number of priests at the various parishes, and in most cases, the younger ones were asked to coordinate and coach CYO teams and clubs because they had such a strong connection with the young people of the congregation. It didn't take long for other sports to be added to the mix, including more subdued competitions such as golf and table tennis.

Table tennis was especially popular in the early days and remained so for decades. Because of its available space, Little Flower was the main venue for table tennis tournaments, with several tables set up in the gymnasium. It was also one of the few sports that allowed for mixed doubles, and while most kids signed up for table tennis as another fun CYO activity, there were those who took the sport more seriously than a friendly game of ping-pong. "Some of those players could be hard-core," offered one CYO staff member.

Chris Cooke, a northside resident, said that he and his brother, Brian, were heavily involved in table tennis tournaments as kids, and he verified the intense level of competition at which they played. The two practiced often

Table tennis was taken more seriously than a friendly game of ping-pong to CYO kids. This shot at the Little Flower Junior CYO clubroom was taken in 1939. *Courtesy of the Indianapolis CYO.*

and became such strong players that they could play with either hand. One night, while playing in a tournament, the brothers made a vow that they wouldn't play with their dominant hand until it couldn't be avoided.

"My opponent ended up with twelve points before I switched hands, and he didn't score again for the rest of the match," he said. "The look on his face was precious after I switched hands. He looked so confused when a moment before he seemed pretty confident. Brian won his division playing with his left hand."

IF YOU BUILD IT…

The popularity of the CYO sports program facilitated the need to create a multifaceted central hub where sporting events could be held. In 1947, a 13.2-acre tract of land was purchased at 1502 West Sixteenth Street to be used as the CYO sports stadium. Frank McKinney was named chairman of the stadium committee and set about collecting funds for development of the property. Construction began in 1948, and after a year's worth of work, the dedication was held on September 12, 1949, during a double-header featuring Cathedral v. Westfield and Sacred Heart v. Carlton-Plainfield.

The CYO athletic field was a boon for the community and a treat for those who remember the beautiful and well-kept stadium, which was far superior to other local fields. There were also extra amenities, which were a nice bonus, as well.

Terry (McDonnell) Wilgus, a 1961 graduate of Scecina Memorial High School, said that the stadium featured plenty of parking, bleachers for the fans and a concession stand, making it a nice facility to visit with your family and friends. "The stadium may not have been as large as some of the fields at the public schools, but it served nicely as the home field for all of the parochial schools and Catholic high schools in the area, and it was centrally located enough that it was easily accessed from all directions," she said.

"I used to love going with my father to the CYO athletic field," said Ed Fillenwarth Jr. He said that he attended many CYO events with his father, especially the football games down at the stadium, where his father served as the announcer for the events. "He did it until I was about in seventh grade and was on the field playing. I guess he didn't feel it was right to be announcing with his son on the field. Perhaps he didn't want to be biased."

As a student at an eastside Catholic grade school, Steve Warren enjoyed caravanning with his team to the CYO field in preparation for

An aerial shot of the CYO Cadet Football Jamboree at the CYO athletic field shows the number of sports participants and spectators who took part in the festivities. *Courtesy of the Indianapolis CYO.*

a big game. From the time he and other athletes on the bus reached Ralph's Muffler Shop on Sixteenth Street, the group began shouting, "We're number one," no matter how the season was going. He said there was a great sense of pride to play on that field, not to mention it was one of the cleanest fields in Indianapolis, devoid of the rocks, dirt and glass that could be found in the municipal fields. "It was also great when the public address system announced your name after a big play. You would hear, 'Tackle by Warren,' or something to that effect. It was a great experience," he said.

Of course, with one field and a large contingency of schools to accommodate, the stadium had scheduling conflicts from time to time. Not only was the stadium used for football games in the fall, but track and field competitions had to be arranged as well. Terry Wilgus said that games were scheduled throughout the week in order to get every team in: "Some of us had to have our games on Thursday nights, some had them on Friday and then there were some games held on Saturday afternoon. We also had the football jamboree in that stadium each year, and it was always a thrill to be out there with the team and have pictures taken. I was even a queen candidate for one of the events they had down there."

A Miss CYO Cadet crowning from 1960. The winner was Sharon Pehlen from the Immaculate Heart of Mary School; her attendants accompany her, with Charlie Hill at the wheel. *Courtesy of the Indianapolis CYO.*

With so many athletic programs on the grade school and high school level vying for field time, the need for additional facilities became more apparent. Parks could be used, of course, for outdoor games such as football, but more schools began adding gym facilities in their remodeling plans, and in 1962, the archdiocese turned over a 13.6-acre property at Perkins and Raymond Streets, on the south side of Indianapolis, to the CYO for use as an additional sporting venue. The property was subsidized by Monsignor Downey K of C Council 3660, which not only held a flag ceremony at the dedication of the field but also helped install two baseball fields, a softball diamond, two football fields, a parking lot and a maintenance building. The additional space afforded the overbooked CYO Stadium some relief. To this day, the Monsignor Downey Athletic Field is still used by a number of CYO athletes.

But it still wasn't enough, and in 1968, 6.5 acres of land was purchased next door to Chatard High School to be used as a neighborhood "green space" and playground. Once again the K of C members, this time Council 3433 of St. Pius X Parish, stepped in to help develop the Ray Katzenberger Jr. CYO North Field, named for a Vietnam War veteran who was killed

A flag-raising ceremony at the Monsignor Downey Athletic Field with the Knights of Columbus, who not only helped to secure the land but also donated their time and energies to making it a playable field. *Courtesy of the Indianapolis CYO.*

Another photo of the flag raising and dedication of the Monsignor Downey Athletic Field, which is still used by the CYO today. *Courtesy of the Indianapolis CYO.*

in action. The field contained a baseball diamond, a softball diamond and a football field. "The field is still an archdiocesan field today, but it is maintained by Chatard and does not have the CYO moniker," Tinder said. "We still use it for lots of events, though."

Gymnasium facilities were also shared by many of the schools during those early days when not every school had a gym or auditorium. Wilgus remembered that Our Lady of Lourdes in Irvington was one of the rare parishes that had a gym of its own (which it loaned for use to other parishes when the need arose), and it also employed a lay faculty member who served as a coach for the school's athletic teams.

"His name was Carl Potenza," Wilgus said. "He was the only lay teacher I had while I was a student at Lourdes. He was in charge of all the team sports, and we felt so fortunate to have our own coach on staff. Prior to him, our grade school kickball team was usually coached by an older daughter of a lady in the parish, but I can't recall having a real coach prior to him."

Over time, more and more schools had their own athletic facilities, and maintaining multiple community fields became cost-prohibitive to the archdiocese. In 1975, the CYO athletic field was sold to a trucking

An early shot of what would become the Ray Katzenberger Jr. North CYO Field. It was named for a Vietnam War veteran and contained a baseball and softball diamond along with a football field. *Courtesy of the Indianapolis CYO.*

Though it is no longer known as the Ray Katzenberger Jr. North CYO Field, the land is still used by the CYO and maintained by Chatard High School. *Courtesy of the Indianapolis CYO.*

company that subsequently sold the property to the Indianapolis Parks Department. Tinder said that with many schools having soccer fields and their own football fields and gymnasiums, the CYO has more athletic sites than ever before. "Every school has a gym. Some have soccer and football fields. Some use the local high school facilities. There's not as much need now for that central location when there are plenty of venues all over the region."

Equal Opportunity

Since its inception in 1930, the CYO prided itself in offering a diverse line of athletic opportunities, not just limited to football, basketball, baseball or boxing but rather one that ventured out into track, golf, swimming and other sport leagues, as well. Unfortunately, the sporting prospects for young ladies were limited in the early days. A few progressive parishes and schools might

Little Flower cheerleaders in the 1950s rooting for their team at the CYO athletic field in downtown Indianapolis. *Courtesy of Little Flower Catholic Church.*

A CYO girls' tennis team. Tennis and cheerleading were some of the few girls' sports organized in the first few decades of the CYO. Some schools offered basketball leagues as well, but many of the female teams were strictly on the intramural level. *Courtesy of the Indianapolis CYO.*

have offered a girls' basketball or volleyball program, but for the most part, cheerleading was one of the few widespread female athletic options.

"Girls just didn't do those kinds of things in the '50s," said Wilgus, a former cheerleader. She explained that despite the World War II–era All American Girl Baseball League making a case for women's sports in the '40s, the postwar years saw a return to traditional thinking about young ladies and assumed that their futures were in the home and not on the playing field.

Wilgus said that she lacked athletic coordination as a young girl and was often chosen last for pickup games in the school playground. "There were so few girls' sports available unless they were on the intramural level," she noted. "No one was overly concerned with physical exercise for a young lady. It wasn't a deliberate discrimination. It was just the way things were done at the time."

Then there was kickball, a game synonymous with parochial schoolchildren in Central Indiana. For many young ladies in area parishes, their childhoods might not have been the same without it. Developed about 1917 by Nicholas C. Suess, the game of kickball proved to be ideal

The championship Holy Trinity kickball team poses for a shot outside of Little Flower after a big win. *Courtesy of the Indianapolis CYO.*

Father Robert Borchertmeyer presenting St. Christopher with its trophy for becoming the City Kickball League champions in the mid-1960s. *Courtesy of the Indianapolis CYO.*

for a schoolyard setting and required very little in the way of equipment. It also enjoyed the same basic rules as baseball, so it was easily understood by all participants and could be organized to accommodate nearly any number of players. In no time it became the dominant schoolyard sport.

"I am convinced that kickball is not only a Catholic game but also a Midwestern game," said Mary Lyn Barnett, a former kickball player with Our Lady of Lourdes. "Outside of Indiana and Ohio, I have never heard the game described in the same way that the CYO plays it. In other areas, if it is available at all, it is usually played on a softball diamond with a rubber ball as opposed to a painted asphalt field and a harder leather ball."

Barnett said that kickball was the sort of sport that enabled girls to become stronger athletes and created camaraderie among young ladies in the archdiocese. "It was as much a part of our lives as plaid jumpers," she noted.

Tinder agreed. "When St. Simon was building their campus on the north side, and the community saw the initial renderings for the property, the first thing they wanted to know was the plans for a kickball diamond," he said.

"It is truly an Indiana parochial school sport," said Fillenwarth, noting that emotions run high when there is a challenge to the time-honored tradition of kickball. He said that several years ago there was a proposal to eliminate the spring kickball season at various parishes in order to accommodate a new soccer league and track team for girls. "That thought didn't get off the ground because kickball coaches and players were so upset. There are some parishes that no longer have two seasons of kickball each year, but those who do play it are passionate about it, and I've heard that there has even been an adult league formed for those who played kickball in grade school and want to continue playing as adults for fun."

Terry Williams was a parishioner at St. Andrews on the city's north side when a conservative pastor eliminated many of the sports programs at her school, including cheerleading and kickball. When the new pastor arrived, the girls clamored to be allowed to have a kickball program, and that became a popular sports option. "Because you didn't need much to get it going, just

St. Simon's kickball team after a tournament at Little Flower Catholic School. Little Flower was the site for many kickball tourneys due to the fact that the eastside parish had room for three kickball diamonds. *Courtesy of the Indianapolis CYO.*

some painted lines on the parking lot, most schools could get a couple of fields going and accommodate several teams. My public school friends were so jealous because they didn't have kickball like we did."

After school, Williams said that she would walk home with her brothers and their friends, change out of her uniform and bike back to the school for practices and games. Mothers with station wagons would provide transportation when the game was held at a neighboring parish, but parental support for kickball was far from the fervor of the "Friday Night Lights."

"There weren't all of the hovering parents around," she explained. "I mean, people were there and they supported us, of course, but there weren't treats for the team, there weren't a lot of kickball moms—they were home making dinner for everyone. Our athletics were fun, but they looked a lot different than they do today."

It's interesting to note that before the 1970s, only one in twenty-seven girls played high school sports on a national level, and there were virtually no college scholarships for female athletes. Universities thought so little of their women's programs that they only allotted about 2 percent of their budgets to female sports and tended to encourage girls to concentrate their endeavors in other areas, such as home economics, nursing and teaching rather than science, innovation and professional sports.

But Title IX legislation changed all of that. In 1972, Title IX affected ten key issues in equality for women and girls, from access to higher education and science to technology and employment, but its impact is often associated with athletics. Title IX required gender equality for both boys and girls in any educational program and demanded that equal funding be appropriated for all players, no matter the sexual category. As a result of this legislation, the variety, opportunity and availability of girls' sports flourished throughout the country and ultimately affected CYO as well.

As a private entity, CYO was never pressured by Title IX legislation to add girls' sports programs and was always willing to add those teams when there was enough interest to warrant them. It is probable that after Title IX, girls became more interested in sports, and therefore demand increased.

"I never felt like the CYO was deliberately discriminatory or anything prior to Title IX, but I think it was more of a case that you can't miss what wasn't available. Still, when the opportunity arose, suddenly there were a number of girls' teams that sprang up throughout the diocese," Wilgus said. "The culture shifted, and girls became more involved with athletics."

"There was a big change at some point," said Williams. "I graduated high school in 1969 and got out of college in 1973, and in that four-year time

After Title IX, girls' sports became more and more prominent in the CYO. Volleyball, basketball, tennis and track became companions to kickball and cheerleading. *Courtesy of the Indianapolis CYO.*

A shot of a 1974 girls' track meet at the CYO athletic complex in Indianapolis. The young lady's identity is unknown. *Courtesy of the Indianapolis CYO.*

span, girls sports exploded. Ladywood had basketball, I do remember that, but after college, I noticed a big change."

With the CYO sports program flourishing, and with both boys and girls signing on to participate, the important thing became finding good people to train and mentor young athletes in order to prepare them for the "thrill of victory and the agony of defeat."

Chapter 5
"Put Me In, Coach!"

They've got to have direction and instruction.
—Ernest "Blackie" Giovannangelo

After-school athletic programs are not without their controversies. Education experts have lamented their purposefulness, the financial burdens on the school systems, both private and public, and the mixed messages sent to student athletes, who are often commended more for what they accomplish on the field than for what they accomplish in the classroom. However, even the heart of the most stoic administrator grows soft when it comes to the relationship between a student athlete and his or her coach. For out of that relationship develops a never-ending bond in which life lessons are shared and intense trust is developed.

One of the reasons that the CYO high school athletic programs proved to be so dynamic is because the organization had programs on the grade school level, not to mention coaches who were committed to their young charges right from the very start. From the earliest years, when coaching responsibilities fell to the young priests of the parish and then branched out into the laity, CYO was blessed to have a number of men and women willing to donate their time and talent to help young people develop their athletic abilities. These coaches provided leadership, familiarity and direction to the children in their care while helping them become contributing competitors and grow into seasoned veterans on the field.

Most were parents themselves, willing to share their love of a game with the next generation, while others were teachers willing to work extra hours

St. Barnabas's basketball team at the Holiday Tourney held at Our Lady of Lourdes. Coaches included Jim Chase (left) and Tom Egold (right). *Courtesy of the Indianapolis CYO.*

and extend themselves to another aspect of the vocation to which they were so dedicated. They gave selflessly of themselves time and time again without any thought to personal reward or pats on the back for their efforts.

From 1961 to 1966, Diane (Hofmeister) Elzroth worked in the CYO office watching the coaches create exceptional programs that brought out the best in student athletes without expecting anything in return. "They helped establish intramural programs and other opportunities on the grade school level so that by the time those kids were in high school, they had been playing for years," she said.

It was an advantage that the public schools simply didn't have. The individual contributions of CYO coaches helped children everywhere find their inner athletic star and offered parents the opportunity to share in their child's athletic ambition, which led to stronger and more active families on the parish level. No matter whether they were male or female, the lessons that coaches imparted to their young players were felt long after the last whistle blew or the last buzzer sounded.

As more and more girls participated in sports, there were more female coaches who served as surrogate mothers and sisters to young ladies during their formative years. Sue Spencer was active in CYO athletics as a student at Holy Spirit grade school on the city's far east side. Before graduating in 1972, she played both kickball and basketball, noting the fun and excitement that she had as a student athlete winning the city tournament that fall and having the team's picture featured in the *Criterion* newspaper. She also said that it was important to be mentored by female coaches such as Roselle Darraugh, who was later honored by the school for her contribution to girls' sports. "She was a wonderful coach and person. She had six children yet found the time to coach both fall and spring kickball seasons, basketball and volleyball for several years," Sue said, noting Darraugh's penchant for instilling in her teams good sportsmanship and respect for opponents. "We always started every game in a huddle saying a prayer, and we all respected her very much. She really meant a lot to us."

"I grew up with a coach for a dad, and I've seen firsthand, many times over, how a parent will try and talk to his or her son without any luck, but

Female coaches, such as Holy Spirit's Roselle Darraugh, made a big difference in the lives of other young female athletes, including Sue Spencer. *Courtesy of Sue Spencer.*

my dad would walk over, put his arm around the player and have the player open up immediately," wrote Internet columnist Sue Poremba, noting that her brother's friends often turned to her father in seeking his perspective and advice for everything from personal issues to troubles with girlfriends. "This is the bond that coaches can forge with an athlete."

LESSONS OF MY FATHER

Like Poremba, Antoinette Maio Burford saw the impact that the leadership of her father, John Maio, had on his athletes over the years he served as a football coach. Many times, former players came up to their "coach" and thanked him for the life lessons he taught them out on the gridiron and told him how much his leadership skills were appreciated and transferred over into their own lives. Burford herself was influenced by her father's leadership

A vintage shot of Christ the King's baseball team. Without caring coaches who were often parish parents or clergy members, the CYO athletic department wouldn't be where it is today. *Courtesy of the Indianapolis CYO.*

skills as an athlete in cheerleading, kickball, basketball and volleyball, ultimately becoming a CYO coach herself.

Burford has dedicated more than twenty years of her life to cheerleading and ten years to kickball, and she said that her father's work ethic is always forefront in her mind. "He taught me that doing your best and working hard in life makes you a better person," she recalled. "My father taught me to never quit. Even if I didn't like a sport, I had to finish out the season and give it 100 percent. Once you quit, you see how easy it is, and you want to do it again and again."

Relying on her faith and the guidance she received not only from her father but also from other coaches, such as Judy McFadden, Burford encourages her athletes at St. Matthew and Holy Angels to give 100 percent on the field and form those lifelong friendships that last off the field as well. She said that she enjoys helping kids participate in a sport that they may not otherwise have the means to do so—helping them learn the game and perform to the best of their ability while making sure that they understand what's really important in life: getting a good education and developing a work ethic that

Our Lady of Mount Carmel players making their presence known at the 1978 Cadet Football Jamboree at Roncalli High School on the south side of Indianapolis. *Courtesy of the Indianapolis CYO.*

will take them as far as they want to go. "It does not matter how great of an athlete you are; if you don't make the grades, you cannot be successful. Education is your ticket to success, and sports gives you the drive and the discipline to make you a success in life," she said.

Mike Archer found a quasi-father figure in his favorite coach, Tom Moorman. Archer loved all sports as a student at Little Flower and longed to play football, basketball and baseball for the eastside school. Being larger than some of the other boys at school and showing a natural aptitude for the hoops, Archer dropped football and baseball quickly and concentrated his efforts on basketball. He competed under a number of coaches, including his own father, Mike Sr.

It wasn't easy to have his father as a coach, even though Archer, who became an all-American athlete in college and today lives in Kentucky, said that he is confident his father felt that he was doing the right thing by contributing his efforts to the program, but the two were constantly at odds. "Tom Moorman became very important to me because when I was going through tough times at home, he would listen to me and give proper advice," Mike said. "I really loved playing for him. He got as much out of me as any coach I played under, and I played for a bunch. He made me feel like I could accomplish anything, and that's half the battle of being a coach. Eventually, I hope to move back to the Indianapolis area in order to make that same kind of difference in a kid's life."

BIG BROTHER IS WATCHING

While some coaches became surrogate parents, others served as cool older siblings for their young charges. As a student at Holy Spirit Catholic School from 1959 to 1967, Greg Bierck spent the majority of his sporting life as a member of the Miramar swim team but took a hiatus from aquatics in order to play basketball with his school's CYO program.

While there were any number of sports programs for kids, including those at the local parks department and the YMCA of Indianapolis, Bierck said that CYO was special, family oriented and something in which he wanted to take part. "The coaches were fathers of the kids themselves, or they were coaches who grew up playing CYO sports and came back to coach the kids in their late teens or early twenties," he said. "Winning was important, but fundamentals, sportsmanship and team play was the real lesson to be learned in the CYO."

Bierck's favorite coach was a young man who coached his basketball team throughout the 1965–66 season before joining the U.S. Air Force. Terry Rogers was in his twenties and eligible for the draft during the turbulent Vietnam era. After coaching the team and moving on to his military duties, Bierck remained in touch with Rogers, writing to him often while he was in the service. "I still have the comment card he gave me after that one basketball season," he said. "To keep a memento like that for the last forty-four years…I think that says something about the caliber of coach he was and what the CYO athletic program meant to me."

Teachers are not known for having time on their hands, but time after time, many have stepped up to the plate, metaphorically, and offered their coaching services to the CYO. Kevin Sullivan was a math teacher at the old St. Simon's Parish on the city's eastside before it changed location and moved north. According to Diane Elzroth, he was a natural teacher and got along well with the kids. "I just thought he was the best," she noted.

Track was a great sport—one could learn endurance and stamina, and with your coach's help, one could always work at your personal best. *Courtesy of the Indianapolis CYO.*

Dawn Till-Fitzgerald agreed. She was a member of the track team that Sullivan coached and said that many kids came out for track, not because they were so interested in the sport but because of the love and respect they had for the coach and the desire they had to work with him: "St. Simon's track team was known as the 'Blue Army' during the years that Kevin was the coach, and for years afterward simply because of the number of kids who would participate. It didn't hurt that we had some talent, too, but to see us streaming across the field at city tournaments and track meets was daunting."

COACH "GENGHIS KHAN"

Today, Kevin Sullivan is the director of Camp Rancho Framasa in Brown County, but he marveled at the memories recalled by one of his athletes. He said that he was humbled to know that he had made such a difference. Sullivan became a coach partially due to his own positive experiences within the CYO athletic program. He was on the St. Simon football, wrestling, basketball and track teams, showcasing his athleticism at the CYO stadium under coaches who helped him condition season after season.

Sullivan said that it was Carl Wagner who got him started in coaching. Wagner was a seventh- and eighth-grade math, science and physical education teacher at St. Simon who also coached the Cadet A volleyball and track teams. "I really had nothing to do with St. Simon in high school, but during my second year at IUPUI, I was feeling very burned out in my chemical engineering major when I was told that Carl needed some help with the track team," he said.

Excited by the prospect of competition over chemistry, he went over to St. Simon, on the far east side of Indianapolis, where he was met by an unruly group of eighth-grade boys that was waiting for him. "Kevin Corcoran hopped off the railing and got in my face, asking, 'What's your name?' I was still a little unruly myself at that age, so I replied, 'Genghis Khan,' and that nickname stuck with me forever."

Sullivan fell in love with the kids and, through coaching, opted to take some education classes, ultimately changing his major to middle school education, with a concentration in math and science. For the next ten years, he said, he became a "Carl Wagner Jr.," helping with the track team and taking over Cadet A volleyball. When he graduated from IUPUI, he was hired by St. Simon to teach junior high math and science after

A wide shot of a well-attended track meet in 1966 at the CYO athletic field. Today track meets are often held on the campus of IUPUI. *Courtesy of the Indianapolis CYO.*

Wagner went on to work for the CYO office. In years to come, he would again help Sullivan make the next move in his life: becoming the director of the CYO camp.

Sullivan said that those he coached became good friends and that few coaching opportunities allow for such a strong bond. "One kid I coached my first year, Paul Haor...we became such good friends that once he was out of high school we were the best men in each other's weddings, and we were inseparable as the volleyball and track coaches at St. Simon...I look back on it, and it was a full-time job coaching track at St. Simon. We had 112 kids on the team, and our practices looked like three-ring circuses—it was very well organized, but there was a lot of activity," he said. "The thing I always hoped to accomplish as a CYO coach is that every kid who came out had the chance to participate. We treated every kid as though they were a superstar, and we played as hard as we practiced. I never got home before six o'clock at night because I would stay after for their other games, such as kickball. I know we kept some kids out of trouble by being so present and so consistent with our mission, message, time and place."

Paying It Forward

Despite their initial meeting, Kevin Corcoran said that Sullivan came into his life at a particularly difficult time—not long after his parents' divorce in 1971. Today's kids are accustomed to single-parent families, but it was a unique situation for that time, and many didn't know what to make of it.

Corcoran was close to his father, a relationship that remains strong to this day, but without the daily "male figure" in his life, he looked to his parish for positive role models. Wagner was one, and not long afterward, Sullivan became another one. Corcoran said that between the two of them, the track team always had coaches whom they could look up to, love and respect. He remains grateful for all that Sullivan shared with him over the years that enabled him to grow and become a better athlete and person.

"Kevin was probably the first person who taught me about strategy, tactics and leadership," Corcoran said. "He was both mentor and friend during my high school years. Many of the life lessons he imparted were delivered through training together as long-distance runners. Through hard work, we both performed well beyond our natural talent on the track—that's the importance of having a good plan and executing it with precision, all of which I learned from him."

Once he was out of grade school, Sullivan continued to mentor, encouraging Corcoran to try out for cross country at Scecina. He pushed Corcoran to break school records (many of which he still holds), and Corcoran said that the lessons of hard work and perseverance have never left him, not to mention having a willingness to give back.

"After Kevin stopped coaching at St. Simon, Doug Price, James Joven and I took over the coaching; we did our best to carry on the school's winning tradition and to be there for the kids (many of whom are now approaching forty!)," Corcoran said. "But Kevin has an undeniable, special gift for relating to young people. He's influenced many, many others through his involvement in CYO sports and Camp Rancho Framasa. By example, he teaches people to believe in themselves and to lead," he added. "That's a gift he gave me that I've done my best to pay forward."

Continuing the Legacy

Through coaching, the CYO knows that it has the opportunity to inspire its young players to be their best, both in school and on the playing field, with a variety of people who have "been there, done that" and have the desire to pass it on to the next generation of athletes. Tinder said that inspiration is worth more than any win that is accumulated during a season. He said it is important for coaches to balance the seriousness with the fun in any given sport.

"My fifth-grade basketball coach, Sue Mills, did that," said Julia Murphy, a current athlete with St. Michael's in Greenfield. "She knew it was my first time playing, and she took the time to explain everything perfectly so I could do my best. She even juggled balls for us to keep it all light and fun. That's the kind of coach you want to have in your life."

Throughout the country, there has been a constant push to provide CYO participants with quality coaching staff that train and inspire young people everywhere. Los Angeles, for example, began using the "Play Like a Champion Today" program geared to helping athletes appreciate the underlying spiritual component in CYO athletics.

Designed by University of Notre Dame coaches and faculty, it is an academic-based model that focuses on the best practices in character and spiritual development of kids. According to an article by R.W. Dellinger, "Play Like a Champion Today" is a program "based on the moral principles of justice, tolerance, cooperation, respect, and solidarity. And it helps children

Christopher Young of Little Flower waits his turn on the bench during a 1998 football game against St. Malachy in Brownsburg. *Author's private collection.*

discover for themselves, as the Catholic Catechism states, the 'nobility and grace that shines through sports experiences.'"

Clark Power, creator of the program, said that coaches are continually reminded that they are ministers to their young charges and that they should always remember that they are there to serve. "Adults attitudes toward youth sports should be 'I'm here to help the child play' and to remember that it's 'only a game,'" he said, according to Dellinger.

Today, the Indianapolis CYO organizes competitions in fourteen different sports for boys and girls to enjoy, from fourth grade through their high school years. There have also been additions to the program that enable coaches to be effective and responsible leaders to the children they are entrusted with, including VIRTUS and other training programs that remind them of their role as a youth minister, leader, teacher and parent. One of the most significant CYO changes over the years is the inclusion of everyone who wants to play, rather than holding tryouts for a select number of available slots.

"We have been told that CYO would be a much better league if we didn't have so many teams, but we refuse to cut," Tinder said. "It's too important to us to have everyone participate and have the opportunity to play. St. Simon, for example, boasts a whopping twenty-eight basketball teams, but that's fine because we want everyone to play. That's what sets us apart."

CHAPTER 6
ONE TIME AT CYO CAMP

Make new friends but keep the old one is silver and the other gold.
—*Camp Song*

Summer camp is a rite of passage for millions of American youngsters and an adventure unlike any other. No matter if they participate in a traditional camp in a picturesque wilderness setting—learning skills such as first aid, horseback riding, handicrafts, archery and canoeing—or a specialty camp with all the comforts of home, summer camp enables children to make new friends while living independently from mom and dad.

The first organized overnight camp was coordinated by Fredrick Gunn and his wife, Abigail, in 1861. The couple served as the headmasters at the Gunnery School in Connecticut and arranged to take a group of students to the wilds of Long Island Sound, where they were able to experience fishing, boating, hiking and sailing. While some children of means had summer homes that provided them an opportunity to experience a rustic retreat, other families were grateful for the chance to send their children to these unique programs, where they could "rough it and live off the land." Many enthusiastic parents saw camp as a way to extend a child's educational experience into the summer, and it also offered a vital component to overall child development.

GETTING AWAY FROM IT ALL

The modern concept of the summer camp came about in the twentieth century when people realized that summer camp not only would benefit the privileged class but should also be accessible to all children, especially those living in the city, who would benefit from a week in the country, breathing fresh air and having the experience of learning survival skills.

The camps were still largely mom and pop operations located in rural spaces along lakefronts. As camp became more affordable for families, more experts began to wax poetically about its benefits to the overall childhood experience. Even Harvard University president Charles W. Eliot said that "[t]he organized summer camp is the most important step in education that America has given the world," according to "History of Summer Camp."

Summer camps, as we know them, really came in to their own during the World War II era and grew exponentially in the years that followed. For children affected by gas rationing and travel restrictions, summer camp gave them the opportunity for a summer "vacation" and the chance to leave behind the harsh realities of the world. Color Wars and Capture the Flag afforded kids the ability to engage in "battle strategies," while survival skills allowed them to feel a kinship to their family members serving overseas. Handicrafts, songs and friendships provided for the fun and the incentive to return in the years that followed and made summer camp a uniquely American tradition that would be copied in other parts of the world.

From the beginning of the CYO movement, camp was part of the experience. The postwar era gave birth to a number of CYO camps, including one of the earliest in the San Francisco Bay area that was a renovated 1930s Boy Scout camp. In 1946, the twelve-acre facility opened to a number of children. That same year, the Archdiocese of Detroit opened its first CYO camp for boys, with a girls' camp following in 1950.

CAMP RANCHO FRAMASA

Central Indiana was no stranger to the camping experience and was already home to several camping facilities, including the Boy Scout reservation Camp Chank-Tun-Un-Gi (renamed Camp Belzer in 1947), which had been established in 1918, as well as the Girl Scout Camp Dellwood, in Wayne Township, which became a popular summer destination for young ladies. In the years following World War II, CYO was also eager to offer

The lake at Camp Rancho Framasa in 1948. The camp was created on land donated by Bert and Julia Dingle. *Courtesy of the Indianapolis CYO.*

camping experiences to its youth that would enable them to become better members of the Christian community through fun and adventure in natural surroundings.

In 1946, Bert and Julia Dingley of Indianapolis answered CYO's prayer and donated 280 acres of property to the archdiocese for the purpose of establishing a CYO camp for the children of Central Indiana. It was believed that this facility might be able to accommodate one thousand young people over a ten-week period throughout the summer. Organizers were confident that attendees would have the time of their lives learning valuable skills and sharing in activities that would enhance their spiritual lives while communing with nature.

The Dingleys reserved the right to name the new CYO facility as part of their donation to the community. They wanted to call the new venture "Camp

Framasa," using a combination of their children's names: Francis, Margaret and Samuella. The original property contained a chaplain's residence, a leader's residence, a caretaker's cabin, bunkhouses and a kitchen, which had been used as a tank repair shop during the war. There was also a dining space and a barn large enough to hold craft and play activities.

Working at a breakneck speed, by June of that year Camp Rancho Framasa was ready for business and hosted a couple of groups that included the Junior Catholic Daughters of America under director Winifred Galvin and St. Philip Neri's Boy Scout Troop under Scoutmaster J. Earl Owens.

Early on, a camp committee was formed to oversee improvements on the site and to seek out any grants that might help offset those costs. Monsignor Albert Busald, pastor at St. Philip Neri, was named chairman of that board, and he was able to secure upgrades through a grant by the Lilly Endowment for a water filtration system and additional money for the construction of a dam. Other upgrades included a chapel, more bunkhouses, shower facilities and a swimming pool.

By offering activities such as hiking, volleyball, handicrafts, the ever popular table tennis and nature studies, CYO camp was designed to help a camper realize his or her importance as a person through opportunities

Camp Rancho Framasa's kitchen and cabin during the camp's first few seasons. The cabin served as a priest's residence. *Courtesy of Camp Rancho Framasa.*

Camp Rancho's chapel. For years, the camp name was simply shortened to "the Ranch" by most campers. *Courtesy of Camp Rancho Framasa.*

to meet and surpass challenges at various levels. According to the CYO handbook, through the camping experience, young people would make new friends and learn to share with others to develop an awareness of the natural world and a respect for the environment. Campers would also feel a deep sense of achievement and accomplishment and develop a sense of individual responsibility within a small group by assisting in decision-making and cooperative activities while helping to build a spirit of cooperation through self-reliance, independence, spiritual growth, action, creativity and magic.

Life Was Great

By Camp Rancho's tenth anniversary, the facility was meeting and exceeding its goal of one thousand campers each summer. Area youngsters couldn't wait to get down to "the Ranch" after hearing their friends talk about how wonderful it all was and about the fun they had as campers. Jan (Beck) O'Brien started going to Rancho in 1950 as a young lady who began her

Left: Janice (Beck) O'Brien (left) and her siblings, Steven Dave and Sonny, pray at the Camp Rancho grotto in 1953. *Courtesy of Jan O'Brien.*

Below: Janice (Beck) O'Brien, when she was eleven, attending the CYO's Camp Rancho Framasa in 1953. *Courtesy of Jan O'Brien.*

weeklong adventure with check-in on a Sunday, followed by nonstop fun until her parents came back to pick her up the following Saturday.

For thirty-five dollars, along with a five-dollar "canteen" charge for snacks, O'Brien had a ball participating in handicrafts, archery, skits and campfire building with other girls from her school, as well as with new friends who shared her bunkhouse. She said that the programming each week was created with a specific age group in mind. Counselors worked hard to offer campers a diversified program taught through participation in outdoor skills, nature study, crafts, sports, conservation (long before "going green" was a global buzzword) and communion/liturgy services designed to attract a variety of campers each summer.

"Going to camp was unique in that a lot of your friends went, too, and we all got to be in the same bunkhouse," she noted. "You met people from all over Indy, and the counselors would come from all over the state. It was the togetherness that made it special, along with being away from home with your friends. You didn't get homesick at all."

When O'Brien first attended Rancho, Mrs. Helen Zapp was the camp director, and Father John Elford was living in the chaplain's residence and serving as the spiritual guide for the week. Mass, of course, was part of the daily activities, and over the course of the week campers developed close relationships with all of the staff and counselors through their activities, as well as the nighttime campfires that were often a highlight of the camping experience. "At campfire we would all sit in rows and wait for the counselors to light a big bonfire. The counselors would teach us songs, they would put on skits, and after the first [Sunday night] campfire, each cabin was responsible for taking turns and putting on skits each evening. They were always hilariously funny," she said.

To this day, O'Brien can easily remember the lyrics to her favorite camp tunes, including "The Acorn Song," "The Lemon Drop Song" and the 1924 novelty favorite, "Does the Chewing Gum Lose Its Flavor on the Bedpost Overnight?" She also remembered Father Elford as a born storyteller who knew how to spin a scary yarn that would leave campers shivering with delight. One such incident concerned the Pioneer Village, which was located down the road from Rancho and was designed for young men contemplating the seminary. On one particular Friday evening, while Father Elford told the story of the famous Indian, Mantisha, whose grave was supposedly located down the lane from the campfire site, a group of boys rode into Camp Rancho on horseback dressed as Indians. "The Indians came through so fast, doing their war whoop and raising their spears, riding on to Mantisha's grave," O'Brien explained. "Father Elford finished his story with a song, and

Guests of the Pioneer Village, adjacent to Camp Rancho, were often included in some activities, including nighttime campfire ghost stories. *Courtesy of Indianapolis CYO.*

it was always exciting to see the campers' faces as the Indians rode through and back out again."

Vicki (Henninger) Hendley said that the staged "scare" was something that continued at Camp Rancho for many years to come. She, too, recalled a similar experience in the '80s when she was a camper. During one particular nighttime campfire, leader Gerard Striby shared the "Legend of Sleepy Hollow" with the group. She said that when he came to the part in which Ichabod Crane meets the Headless Horseman, someone rode through on horseback in full costume…sans head. "I almost peed my pants," she laughed. "Camp was wonderful for someone like me who was shy. The counselors there really helped me overcome my shyness and have fun in the process."

WE JUST HAD TO GO

CYO director Ed Tinder said that attending camp was, and is, a life-changing experience for many campers. In some cases, those who might not otherwise have had the means to attend camp were able to go through the

One of the big draws to life at camp Rancho Framasa was the equine program, according to many former campers, including Kim Morey Testor. *Courtesy of Camp Rancho Framasa.*

philanthropy of others who saw the benefit that CYO camp had on a child. That was certainly the case for Kim (Morey) Tester.

After her parents' divorce, Tester and her family faced many economic struggles throughout her grade school years. At one point, an employee of Catholic Social Services became acquainted with the family and arranged for Tester's older brother, Kevin, to attend Camp Rancho on scholarship when he was about nine years old. When he returned home after his week at the Ranch, he raved about his experiences in archery, swimming, fishing, campfires and horseback riding. Tester said that after hearing his stories, she and her sister, Denise, just had to go to camp as well.

"The thing that piqued my interest was horseback riding," she remembered. "My mother looked into scholarships for us, as well as my younger brother, Josh, when he was old enough to attend. We were at Camp Rancho Framasa on and off into our preteen years, and if it weren't for the generosity of others, my siblings and I would never have had a camp experience."

Tester's personal photos from her time at camp show a young girl enjoying trail rides with her friends, attending coed dances and posing with her friends

Campers at the Ranch trying to start a fire the old-fashioned way. Activities at the ranch included a number of survival skills and handicrafts. *Courtesy of Camp Rancho Framasa.*

Hanging out with the pack mules and making friends with others was part of the CYO camp experience. *Courtesy of Camp Rancho Framasa.*

all with an ear-to-ear grin on her face. So influential was her time at Rancho that she longed to grow up, major in equine studies and become a horsewoman as an adult, all thanks to the counselors she encountered each summer. She even served as a horse specialist when she became a junior counselor. "It was a lot of work, but I loved it. I learned how to feed the horses, brush them out and put on their saddles and bridles," she said. "Once, when I was brushing a horse out, it pinned me to the side of the stall while stepping on my toes. When I finally pushed it off, it bucked me in the thigh. It was painful, but it didn't keep me from wanting to continue working with them."

In addition to her four-legged companions, Tester loved the skits that the counselors put on for the campers, as well as the mottoes that were adopted and placed on wooden discs to be hung in the main pavilion. She recalls learning some of her favorite childhood melodies at camp, such as "Magdelena, Hegdelena," "Three Sharp-Toothed Buzzards," "Have You Ever Seen a Turtle?" and the 1960s Peter, Paul and Mary tune, "Old Stewball," about a racehorse that only drank wine. As a teacher and a mother, she has passed on those songs to her daycare kids and even sang a few to her sons when they were little.

"Never experiencing camp would have been a tragedy, as I believe that CYO camp is largely responsible for the positive characteristics that each of us possess and our way to overcome the challenges of our parents' divorce and our resulting poverty," Tester said. "Camp shaped us into who we are. Responsibility, flexibility, determination and confidence are all traits I can contribute to the camp experience."

Sharing the Experience

It is a tribute to the counselors who gave of their time and talent that so many campers longed to come back and share the experience with future summer groups when they were old enough. O'Brien said that the first step in becoming a counselor was to get involved in Rancho's Counselor in Training (CIT) program. The only payment was a free week of camp, but it gave junior counselors the chance to learn the ropes and start mentoring the next generation of Rancho campers. (Senior counselors received a small stipend for their work.) She longed for the day when she could become one of the "cool" counselors whom she admired, even though it meant getting harmless pranks pulled on you, such as having your bed "short-sheeted."

Campers enjoying their week at camp by taking part in waterfront activities, such as canoeing. *Courtesy of Camp Rancho Framasa.*

O'Brien was a counselor in the bunkhouse but eventually passed her Water Safety Instruction and was put in charge of swimming lessons for new campers at the pool. Between 1957 and 1962, O'Brien was a counselor, while Cecilia Mootz was the camp director. Father Elford was still on hand, of course, and many of her breaks between camping sessions were spent in Nashville at the laundromat, cleaning her clothes for the following week and trying to wash off all of the red clay dust that had caked everything. "After all, camp was located on Clay Lick Road," she laughed.

"I met so many great gals from other Catholic high schools in Indianapolis, and we are still good friends to this day. The campers looked up to the counselors, and it gave you such a wonderful feeling that you were doing something important for these kids," she said.

For O'Brien and Tester, like other counselors, becoming a counselor at Rancho was never about the money but rather the opportunity to share the camp experience and help other campers have the time of their lives.

Camp Christina

Thanks to the success of Camp Rancho and the number of attendees each summer, in 1961 CYO received another tract of land in Brown County that was geared to offer young women additional camping facilities. It would eventually be a coed camp, but it was always a little more primitive than the Ranch. It was called Camp Christina, and O'Brien remembered that several counselors from Rancho Framasa were selected to help "build" the new site and get it ready for its first season.

Camp Christina had the same mission as Rancho; however, there were only a few permanent buildings on the property, including a chapel, which had a room for Father Elford, and a storeroom for the perishables. Other than that, it was a makeshift, live-off-the-land kind of camp in which these early employees had to use their ingenuity to build a shower house from canvas and posts, as well as rig a shower head to the water supply. "We had a lot of talent," O'Brien noted.

The chow hall at Camp Christina, another CYO camp located in Brown County and established by many counselors who worked at Camp Rancho. *Courtesy of Indianapolis CYO.*

Tents were erected on cement foundations and could accommodate eight to ten people per structure, depending on the season, with a cooking tent between them in order to help campers learn to make their meals from scratch while cooking over a fire. One of O'Brien's favorite meals was the Hobo Hamburger. "I still fix those at home today," she said.

Due to the rugged nature of Camp Christina, some of the activities that could be held onsite at Rancho were located offsite at Camp Christina, such as swimming. Campers were more than willing to board the "old camp bus"—Rancho being in possession of the "new camp bus"—and head to Gnaw Bone Camp for waterfront activities. The trip alone could be perilous, according to O'Brien, who remembered Father Elford imploring all riders to "take a breath" so that the bus would make it to the top of the hill. Sometimes it worked and sometimes it didn't. "If we didn't make it, we all got off the bus, and Father Elford would get the vehicle over the top of the hill, then yell, 'Everyone back on!'" she said.

Terry Williams was another camper from Rancho who ultimately became a counselor at Christina, riding in the "seatless" bus and sleeping with the sides drawn up on her tent, which attracted neighboring donkeys to stop by and

The lakefront that was used for water activities at Camp Christina. More primitive than Camp Rancho, Christina holds special memories for those who spent their summers there. *Courtesy of Indianapolis CYO.*

visit. One memory that stands out, though, was using the chapel as a "port in a storm" one night when a tempest drove the campers from their tents.

"It was just a cinder block building, and there was this little room in the back set aside as the chapel," she said. "There weren't even any kneelers in there, and any time we had Mass in there we had to use sit-upons, so you can imagine what it was like to huddle in there together against the storm. Still, it wasn't like we really minded. I loved Christina, and I loved how primitive it was. I think that is what made it even more special."

Despite roughing it, campers and staff developed a fondness for Camp Christina, often becoming emotional at the end of the week and not wanting to return home. No one was ever ready for the fun to end, and O'Brien took a special responsibility for making sure that the campers got as much out of their experience as they could. More often than not, she felt that she got even more from them: "As a counselor, you wanted it to be the best week of their life so that they could tell Mom and Dad that camp was great and that they want to go back. Feelings for camp are often hard to explain, but they were special feelings to be sure."

Like friendships forged at Rancho, campers at Christina maintained lifelong relationships with those they met during the week. O'Brien said that Camp Christina holds a special place in her heart thanks to one particular set of campers: a group of Hispanic girls, sponsored by local families and attending Ladywood Academy on the northside of Indianapolis (today the home of Cathedral High School). In 1962, the girls' families sacrificed everything to help the young ladies escape from Castro's Cuba and come to the United States, where they were able to attend Catholic school and go to camp.

"They were in my tents, which were called 'Chigger City,' and they were the neatest group of high school girls. They had Hispanic phrases they used in camp, and no one knew what they were talking about, but they were funny phrases, and they would laugh so much. I still remember their names and wonder where they are today," O'Brien recalled. "It was wonderful to be a part of their lives."

However, the good times could last only so long. After the 1990 summer season, a feasibility study was conducted on Camp Christina, and it was concluded that it was becoming too expensive to operate two camps under the CYO banner. Though it was known how much Christina meant to the men and women who were campers and counselors at the facility, including the memories that were made on the grounds, the CYO decided that it was time to sell Camp Christina and use the proceeds to improve Rancho. "That

A liturgical celebration at Camp Christina in later years. Many were sad when the camp was sold in order to make improvements to Rancho, but the CYO summer fun continues to live on. *Courtesy of Indianapolis CYO.*

was hard, and it wasn't a popular decision," Sullivan acknowledged. "We didn't want to do it, and we knew it was home to many campers, but despite looking for ways to make it work, in the end it made more sense to sell it."

"We still partner on programs with the man who bought Christina, and I am proud to say that he is doing great things down there." said Kevin Sullivan, current director of Camp Rancho Framasa.

THE SUMMER FUN CONTINUES

Sullivan said that CYO camp was the site for many "firsts" in his life—horseback riding, archery, catching that first fish and other developmental milestones were all part of the camp experience. Of course, by the time he was in college, it had been years since he really thought about camp until his mentor, Carl Wagner, made yet another suggestion that would change his life forever. "He said, 'You should work at CYO camp; they always need guys. You're older, and you have a bus driver's license,'" Sullivan said.

He applied for and got the job, which paid a whopping ninety dollars per week, and he spent the next three summers serving as a counselor and bus driver. Like O'Brien, he knew all too well how the campers treated their counselors with good-natured pranks. One camper, Bobby Heidenreich, was part of what Sullivan called the "best/worst" group ever.

"That group drove me crazy—tied me to my bed, kept me up all night, pranked me with buckets of water above doors; they were terrible and awesome at the same time!" Sullivan said. "Bobby came to camp on a scholarship, which was the only way he would have gotten there. Once he got older, he became a counselor and he even met his wife Shannon Swisher at camp!"

Heidenreich graduated from Scecina High School in 1988 and joined the military, eventually serving in an engineering unit in the National Guard. Sullivan said that he got a call one day from his former camper, who offered to have his unit come to Rancho and construct an amphitheater for the facility.

"The beautiful Pines Amphitheater at Rancho was built by Bobby and his unit. Here was a kid that really gave back to camp. Bobby and Shannon are very good friends of ours now, and our kids have become friends with

A group of male Camp Rancho campers from an undated photo. Many of these young men would go on to have children who would also attend the camp. *Courtesy of Indianapolis CYO.*

their kids. I have heard so many great stories of kids who have been granted camping scholarships and attended camp who might not have attended otherwise," Sullivan said. "This kind of generosity seems to follow them throughout their lives."

While a counselor, Sullivan was able to institute many new activities, including gold panning, archaeological digs, making totem poles and other ideas that became part of the fabric of the camping experience, but he said that it is the St. John Bosco philosophy of being among the children and keeping camp camper-centered that makes it an experience that multiple generations have enjoyed over the years.

"We have a great facility, but our staff has always been what sets us apart from other camps," he said, noting that each summer about 2,000 campers come to Camp Rancho Framasa, and about 3,500 come through each school year for various events. "We make the camper *first*, we put their needs ahead of our needs and we listen to them. Some campers have never really had an adult listen to them."

In 1985, Sullivan was asked to take over as the development director of Camp Rancho, and he accepted, although he was still on staff at

Female Camp Rancho campers from 1954. Camp executive director Kevin Sullivan said that many campers grow up to be counselors, send their kids to camp at Rancho and continually give back throughout their lives. *Courtesy of Indianapolis CYO.*

St. Simon and coaching in his spare time. For a while, being the camp director remained a summertime gig, but eventually he moved down to Brown County when the job became full time in the mid-1990s. "I've been here ever since," he said.

Sullivan said that although many years have gone by since Camp Rancho was opened, the spirit remains for the campers who attend each year. He said that the CYO program, whether it is camp, sports or cultural activities, is about relationships with one another and fostering a faith-filled experience. Pranks are still played on counselors, and kids still come back to serve as employees once their camper days are done, he said. "Kids are still kids, and bringing them to live in a community-type setting still works. It breaks down the barriers, and kids become converts of building relationships. They see it work and believe in it, staff and campers alike."

CHAPTER 7
TO AMUSE THE MIND AND AROUSE THE SPIRIT

What will you think of next?
—Cardinal Mundelein

Summer camp, parish chapters and youth sports aside, the vast array of CYO activities throughout Central Indiana can be attributed to those who saw a need and created the opportunity to fulfill the purpose of the Catholic Youth Organization. According to the CYO twenty-fifth anniversary edition of the annual activities report, "It remains for us…to continue to build upon their work, to think continually of the needs of youth and how they might best be cared for, continuing what needs to be continued and initiating those new projects which youth's needs demand."

Though there were many people who worked diligently to create new frontiers for CYO, one name stands above them all: William "Bill" Sahm, who served as the executive director of the program from 1954 until his death in 1973.

"My dad was bigger than life," said William Sahm Jr., who is the current president of Bishop Chatard High School on the city's northside. In an interview with the *Criterion*, he tried to put into words the kind of influence his father had on the organization, as well as the Indianapolis community, and commented that he knows how a faith-based community was committed to a young person's life. "He was the head of the CYO, but he was involved in so many other organizations. I grew up following him around to CYO events, going to communion breakfasts. I had all those wonderful Catholic experiences."

Fillenwarth said that Sahm was the first full-time employee of the CYO to his knowledge and that Sahm's enthusiasm and energy for the program is what set him apart. "Everything that he attended to, he brought his enthusiasm, and that energy and enthusiasm touched everyone around him."

Diane Hofmeister Elzroth, who worked in the CYO office, said that Sahm was a man of vision who didn't hesitate to offer new and popular programming outside of the traditional athletic opportunities previously enjoyed by CYO members. "He was a remarkable man with a lot of interests, and he deserved a lot of credit for building so many programs within the Central Indiana CYO program."

Make a Joyful Noise

The CYO Songfest was just one of those programs. Inspired by his love of music and a stint with the venerated Notre Dame Glee Club, Sahm looked to encourage more musical programs for Catholic youth under the CYO banner. "He loved to sing," said Elzroth. "When it came to identifying more opportunities for kids, he had a great administrative mind and plenty of vision."

Music teachers in a Catholic school setting often extol the spiritual benefits of a melody-based curriculum: when you sing, you pray twice. Of course, early academic ensembles hardly resemble the *Glee*-inspired show choirs of recent years. Actually, glee clubs and choral groups can be traced back to 1787 London, where the first named glee club was initiated at the Harrow School. The popularity of such clubs grew throughout the late eighteenth and early nineteenth centuries, and they crossed the "pond," where they found a place in many American Ivy League schools. Some of the oldest glee clubs in the United States include the Harvard Glee Club, the University of Michigan Glee Club, the Cornell University Glee Club, the Amherst College Glee Club and the Rutgers University Glee Club.

At Sahm's own alma mater, the Notre Dame Glee Club was founded in 1915 and enjoys the reputation of being one of the finest all-male collegiate vocal ensembles. In the years since its inception, more than two thousand men have lent their voices to the club. In 1954, the Senior CYO Glee Club was formed. This ensemble performed several concerts and made informal appearances around the area under the direction of Father Thomas Carey and Father Lawrence Frey. Other music programs followed suit, and by 1957, the first CYO Songfest was held at Butler University's

The 1967 Songfest was bigger than big, with six thousand voices crowding Butler University's Hinkle Fieldhouse. Jan O'Brien said that every school participated and that there was no sheet music allowed. *Courtesy of the Indianapolis CYO.*

Hinkle Fieldhouse. The Songfest featured singers from the student bodies of thirty-nine Catholic schools. There were as many as 6,900 sixth, seventh, and eighth graders participating in the Songfest and about 8,000 people in the audience.

Miss Loretta Martin was an early director of the Children's Chorus during the choral music festival before her death in 1959. She was loved and respected by the children she mentored for the first two years of the Songfest, and she remained committed to the event even after she became ill, listening to the Songfest via a special telephone connection. That same year, heavyweight boxing champ Floyd Patterson made a surprise appearance at the event, to the delight of all in attendance.

In the 1960s, Father Edwin Sahm, chairman of the Archdiocesan Music Commission, directed the Songfest, along with Mr. Edward Krieger of St. Joan of Arc and Father Thomas Briedenback of St. Catherine's. The Songfest included selections of popular and sacred music, along with

A large view of the 1967 Songfest shows the vast number of participants, as well as some of the eight thousand spectators. *Courtesy of the Indianapolis CYO.*

patriotic favorites, to the delight the attendees. March 1960 saw the advent of the Cadet Instrumental Music Contest, which included a variety of performances, from ensemble groups to chamber combos, piano soloists and even accordion quartets. Thanks to Sahm's vision, every child was given the opportunity to share their God-given musical skills with others.

"The Songfest was wonderful!" Jan (Beck) O'Brien said. "All of those voices of the grade school children, filling one side of the Butler Fieldhouse, and everyone singing in unison—it was an unbelievable sound!" O'Brien also credits Sahm with the idea to have a music program, and when the opportunity was presented to her class in the sixth, seventh and eighth grades, she couldn't wait to get involved. One advantage of singing in the festival was missing school in order to practice at Butler. "Of course we had to learn the song by heart…no sheet music to look at, and what made it so cool also, was getting to take buses to Butler Fieldhouse just like the high school kids did for the sectional games…we all thought we were the big time."

One song that stands out for O'Brien during her Songfest days was "The Happy Wanderer." She said that it sounded so good to hear all of the voices lower and build into a crescendo. She said it was her favorite song of the festival. "It was truly a spectacular event. We all had to dress alike: white tops and navy blue bottoms. It was a big deal at the time."

But the musical fun did not end there. The annual CYO talent contest, beginning in 1954, was a highlight of summertime activities. Groups and individual performers from a number of parishes would gather to show off their unique talents long before *The Gong Show* or Piers Morgan of *America's Got Talent* could squelch their ambition. Connie Eaton of St. Philip Neri was an outstanding individual during several years of competing in the talent show. In 1960, 1962 and 1963, she took first place in the variety division, but in 1961 she scored "Best Act" in the show. The Cobras were a song and dance combo from Holy Name who knew how to raise the roof off Chartrand High School with their act, including steps that made the Beatles' moves look like "refugees from the Soldiers and Sailors home," according to the twenty-fifth anniversary annual report.

The 1968 Junior Talent Contest winners, with their priest moderator, proudly display their trophies. *Courtesy of the Indianapolis CYO.*

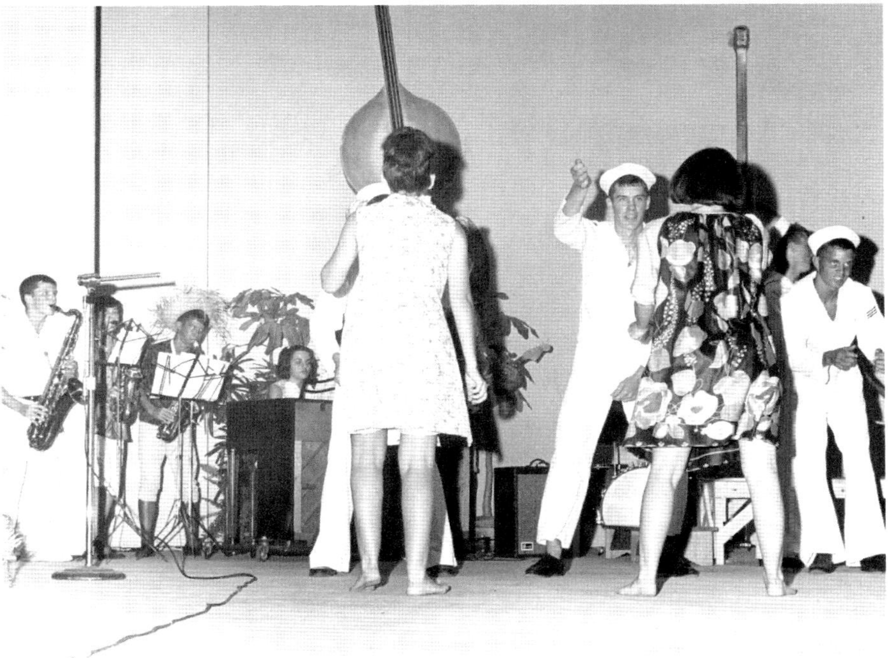

Folks from Holy Name perform a medley from *South Pacific* during a talent contest in 1965. *Courtesy of the Indianapolis CYO.*

Parishes eventually had the opportunity to invest in comprehensive music programs of their own, and suddenly they had the space to accommodate public performances of school choirs and local talent shows. Larger events went by the wayside. However, in the musical scheme of things, one program remains: the CYO Cadet Music Festival, held each year at Bishop Chatard High School. Nearly one thousand musicians and vocalists compete at this annual music contest that end with the CYO Honors Music Recital. Categories for the music festival include instrumental, vocal and piano, performed by students from the fourth to eighth grades.

Raindrops on Roses

Vicki Henninger Hendley was in the fourth grade the first time she competed in the music festival singing, with classmate Dede Esslinger, "My Favorite Things" from *The Sound of Music*. She said the two of them spent hours during sleepovers, choir rehearsals and recess practicing their song, along with the little movements they made up to go along with the lyrics. Fully prepared to knock the judges' socks off, the duo was chagrined to hear another competitor singing the same song, and they were suddenly hit with a case of nerves. "We looked at each other nervously, looked at our moms and ran out into the hallway to rehearse what we thought we had 'in the bag' only twenty minutes beforehand," she said.

Hendley said that the stress levels were high and that the girls had to be reminded several times to remember to relax. Both were worried about everything from forgetting the lyrics to forgetting the movements that might help a little in improving their performance; they would either be a big hit or fail miserably. They didn't need to worry so much: the duo won first place for their vocal performance, and Hendley said it was one of her proudest moments as a vocalist: "I learned that you can still wow the judges and the crowds by performing a popular selection and staying true to your

First-place award ribbons from the Archdiocesan Cadet Music. Vicki (Henninger) Hendley won first place for her rendition of "My Favorite Things" from the *The Sound of Music* in the mid-1980s. *Author's private collection.*

St. Pius X students show off their musical skills during the 1963 music contest. *Courtesy of Indianapolis CYO.*

interpretation of the piece. I was wrong to worry or to be intimidated by anyone or anything else. You simply have to do your best."

Ed Tinder, executive director of the Indianapolis CYO, said there that is a little secret to the music festival most performers never realize. "No one takes a third-place ribbon," he said. "We make sure that we let the judges know that the kids need a first- or second-place win so that they have that sense of accomplishment after their hard work."

"I didn't know any of that," Hendley said, with a laugh. "I just knew that I wanted to sing my heart out like I never had before."

All the World Is a Stage

The CYO Board of Directors was diligent when it came to seeking various creative outlets for its young membership. No matter where a particular artistic talent may lie, it would not stay hidden for long. The Central Indiana CYO was determined to let every light shine.

Casts involved with the one-act play contest greet one another outside of the auditorium. The one-act plays were a great opportunity to get CYOers together and help them learn the craft of theater. *Courtesy of Indianapolis CYO.*

In 1951, the first one-act play contest was held, with subsequent annual performances showcasing the best and brightest thespians in the Circle City. The plays ranged from comedy to drama, with individual awards being given for outstanding actors and actresses in each division. All in attendance were impressed by the level of professional performances that were staged.

During her high school years, Terry Williams took part in several one-act play competitions at St. Andrew's Parish. She said that there wasn't as much of an opportunity to perform in dramas at Chatard High School, and as a self-described "frustrated actress," the One-Act Play Festival allowed troupes to perform several times and hone their craft through an elimination process spanning several weeks.

The mid-1960s saw the rise of a number of impressive groups, including St. Margaret Mary in Terre Haute, which was awarded three consecutive titles, including one for its presentation of "The Birthday of the Infanta" by Oscar Wilde. Our Lady of Lourdes also became the first parish to win both divisions in the one-act play competition under the direction of Father John Minta and Mrs. Howard J. McDavitt.

St. Andrews's one-act company fell under the direction of Rosalyn Gale, and it won the competition in 1968 for its performance of *The Cleanest Town in the West*. In addition, Williams and her friends staged several comedies and melodramas in parishes around the city with stages on which the performances could be showcased.

"We had big casts, like about ten to eleven people, and our parents would help get the costumes ready for our performances, which were held at parishes that had stages, such as St. Michael, St. Catherine and Little Flower," Williams said. "There weren't many scenes, usually just three, so it was manageable. The judges would watch us and then announce who won, and the winners would advance to the big round at Roncalli in early April."

In order to win, Williams said parish groups had to beat out about twelve other groups in the category. Gale was a big fan of western melodramas, and Williams was always willing to jump on stage and refine her character. "I loved everything about it, and I even won the Best Actress award. I

A ghoulishly good time was had by this one-act cast, moderated by Father Dave Brandon in the 1970s. *Courtesy of Indianapolis CYO.*

remember in one of the plays, I was the saloon broad who was kind of a Mae West type—a tough gal with a kind heart, [that] kind of thing."

Williams said that the production called for numerous props and backdrops throughout the show, and during one scene she was supposed to be knocked out just as the lights went out. When the lights went back up, it was to appear as if she had come to, but unbeknownst to the audience, she was really knocked out after hitting her head on a concrete block behind her.

"I was so woozy when I did come back, and I later heard someone say that it was the most realistic acting they ever saw," she said, laughing at the memory of it all. "I ended up out of school with a concussion, but I got that Best Actress award. I hope it wasn't just because of that ending scene. It was a fun thing for us kids to be involved in, practicing two nights a week and then showcasing our work for everyone. There were some really talented kids in the groups, and it gave us so much confidence. I just loved acting."

Creativity, Style and Presentation

Performance art was a great diversion for young musicians and thespians, but the mid-1950s saw the birth of a number of other creative outlets for children in the CYO. The cadet Hobby Show gave young crafters, artists and collectors the chance to show off their skills in categories such as kit crafts, skilled crafts, fine arts, collections, sewing and baking. Hobby Show entries were always unique and imaginative. It might be a favorite family recipe or an elaborate collection of stamps, baseball cards or other hard-to-find items, not to mention artistic efforts in a number of mediums. Winners on the parish level were invited to the Citywide Hobby Show to compete against the best of the best in the archdiocese. "The Hobby Shows were great because there was always a wide range of entries," said Dawn (Till) Fitzgerald.

Hobby Shows might have attracted a great number of entrants, and entries for both boys and girls, but events such as the Junior Style Show and baking competition clearly celebrated home economics and were geared for the future homemakers of America.

In 1950, only one-third of the women in the country were actively engaged in work outside of the home. Some might have held a job for a brief time between high school (or college) and marriage, and as previously noted, few girls were tearing up the sports arenas in the same numbers as boys. At many high schools, young men were involved in "shop" class, while

A shot of the many displays at the CYO Citywide Hobby Show. From skilled crafts to baking, sewing and fine arts, young people had a chance to showcase their skills. *Courtesy of Indianapolis CYO.*

This 1963 entry in the skilled crafts division is of a car built by James Whittenmore from St. Joan of Arc. *Courtesy of Indianapolis CYO.*

The 1962 baking division winner at the CYO Citywide Hobby Show. The Hobby Show competition starts on the parish level and moved to the city rounds a few weeks later. *Courtesy of Indianapolis CYO.*

A 1965 winner in the CYO Hobby Show sewing division from St. Lawrence School on the northeast side of the city. *Courtesy of Indianapolis CYO.*

girls were shuffled off to the home economics room, where they were taught to cook, sew and prepare for life as a wife and mother. The movie *Mona Lisa Smile*, starring Julia Roberts, drives this point home as she witnesses a number of Wellesley girls take classes in elocution and poise while learning how to set the perfect table, raise the ideal children and look great at the same time. In that climate, it was a forgone conclusion that, even with a college education, a woman's real career began after securing her "MRS. Degree."

CYO sought to include young ladies in its many programs, which accounts for the inclusion of events that would have appealed to young ladies at the time. The style show was designed not to be a commentary on traditional male and female roles but rather to give young ladies the chance to show off their personal style.

The first Junior Style Show was held in 1955 to kick off the year. Young ladies, inspired by the postwar "New Look" styles of Dior, sewed and modeled their personal brand of haute couture to the delight of all in attendance. The luxurious fabrics and gorgeous styles of the time were evident in the divisions, which included skirt and blouse, sportswear, tailored dress, tailored suit, party dress and formal dress divisions. As many as two hundred young ladies competed in the style show in a given year, representing dozens of parishes in the area.

"A lot of girls sewed at the time, so that wasn't unusual," said Williams. "Home Ec wasn't a required course, so some learned in school, while others learned from their mothers. There wasn't the clothing turnover that we have today. We didn't have malls. We had Block's and L.S. Ayres. I don't know many girls who didn't learn to make their own A-line shifts or other creations because we just didn't have a lot of clothes."

Greg Bierck was in the first grade when he was invited to take part in the parish style show circa 1959. He modeled a baseball uniform in a walk down a makeshift runway in Holy Spirit's gymnasium, with a spotlight on his face that prevented him from seeing the assembled crowd. He said it was a good thing that he couldn't see the crowd, otherwise the nerves from being in front of so many people might have stopped him in his tracks.

"I might not have gone through with it," he said. "I remember changing in room 1, which was my classroom at the time. That seemed really strange to me. I honestly don't remember if the whole thing was a CYO event or not, it was just another one of those money-making things that we did for the school."

Vintage photos of the style show era indicate that those who took top prizes in their respective categories were accomplished seamstresses who

Participants in the 1957 CYO Style Show created their own ensembles and modeled them for attendees. There was also a dance held in conjunction with the style show so that the pretty party dresses wouldn't go to waste. *Courtesy of Indianapolis CYO.*

Competitors in the formalwear division getting ready to take their turn on the runway during the CYO Style Show. *Courtesy of Indianapolis CYO.*

were deserving of the honors. In 1958, for example, Mary Ellen Benedetto of St. Christopher and Janet Srebalus of St. Pius X were both in the formal dress division. Benedetto went on to graduate from Marian College, teach school and become a member of the CYO office staff. Srebalus eventually entered the Maryknoll convent and became known as Sister David Jerome. In the 1960s, winners included Rita Doyle of Holy Name, Linda Speth of Sacred Heart, Patty Able of St. Mark and Connie McIntyre of St. Gabriel, for her tailored suit creation.

Coupled with the style show and dance, according to Williams, was the baking competition (it is unclear if these events were always held together or if they were separated in some years.) While today's contenders on *Hell's Kitchen* or *Cake Boss* may not be threatened by the wares presented by contestants in the CYO event, it was a very popular competition for bakers, as well as the lucky judges, who were able to sample all of the entered goodies.

Local cafeterias at area parishes were the venue for the competition, which drew as many as 350 participants annually during its heyday. Young ladies baked up a storm for the glory of their parishes with cakes, pies,

Mary Grace LaRoche of St. Roch shows off her winter garb during the 1965 spring style show, the proceeds of which went to fund other CYO activities. *Courtesy of Indianapolis CYO.*

cookies, quick breads and yeast breads. The goods were then auctioned at a dance, attended by 500 or more, with all proceeds going to the Junior Youth Council's treasury.

Williams said that she entered the baking competition with homemade bars that would hardly dethrone Martha Stewart as the "Queen of Domesticity," but she said the baking competition wasn't about presentation or exotic ingredients but rather instead focused on taste, having fun and competing with your friends. "Maybe I was involved in so much because I was very competitive at the time and was willing to compete in anything and everything: table tennis, kickball, baking competitions—it just gave us something to do that helped us stay connected to our parish and build upon those friendships that began there."

"It was a very Catholic world back then. You had your sports, your camps and hobbies, all within the confines of the parish and diocese," said Diane Elzroth. "There was this feeling that you had to do things within the church, and now children have more opportunities and more freedom to mix with others outside of the parish community."

BLINDED BY SCIENCE

Many of the CYO events that were at one time very popular have gone by the wayside over the years due to myriad offerings now available to young people outside of their parishes and schools. Also, the lack of participation in the events and the amount of time and energy it would take to pull off a large-scale archdiocesan event has limited the number of CYO programs. Some, such as the Hobby Show, still occur on the parish level, while others, such as the Quiz Bowl, have morphed into the Academic Olympics and high school Brain Game teams, but one event that still draws a good sized crowd, and multiple generations, is the CYO Science Fair.

Science fairs have been around longer than some might imagine. In 1928, years before students waxed about the benefits of solar energy or demonstrated the effects of air pressure by using a coke bottle and a hard-boiled egg, the American Institute in New York City organized the first "Industrial Fair," full of innovative adult-inspired exhibits, including the iron plow but also a black veil that had been created, supposedly, by an eight-year-old girl. After that exhibition, the institute regularly sponsored children's fairs that highlighted young people's scientific efforts. It is from these fairs that the modern "science fair" was born.

Two students from St. Joseph at the 1968 CYO Citywide Science Fair showing off their project on the human eye. *Courtesy of Indianapolis CYO.*

The movement and popularity of the science fairs grew throughout the 1940s and 1950s, according to "History of Science Fairs": "The first National Science Fair was held in Philadelphia with 13 regional fairs participating. In 1964, finalists from 208 affiliated fairs in this country and abroad participated in the National Science Fair International in Seattle, Washington."

The projects on display encompassed the best efforts of 947,000 young people who had competed in local fairs associated with the larger event. For the CYO, science fairs allowed students to show off their knowledge in both the natural and physical sciences with an emphasis on the scientific method and creativity. Junior high grades were often required to participate in the local science fair in order to gain practical experience in problem solving and presentation.

Greg Bierck was passionate about the science fair as a youngster and remembers that it was a big deal in the parish community. He said the road to the state-level science fair began in science class, where the sisters helped

Judges of the CYO Science Fair have to know what kinds of questions to ask in order to determine if the student has extensive knowledge on their particular project. *Courtesy of Indianapolis CYO.*

their students choose their projects and then mentored them through their progress and through those first steps.

Relying on his interest in paleontology, Bierck said that he knew that his material backward and forward when he was instructed by Sr. Marie Leon to present his project to the class before the competition. "Most kids, I think, had to come up with something and just knew enough to get them through the assignment. I had a true interest in my topic," he said, noting that it made a difference compared to the projects that seemed to have more than their fair share of parental "help."

He said many of the kids hated the required event, but he enjoyed every minute of it, especially when his mother took him to the Children's Museum, where he negotiated with Mr. Cassidy for the loan of a mastodon jawbone and teeth to be used in his display. His mother had to put down a twenty-five-dollar deposit on the items, which were later returned.

"I won for my paleontology exhibit locally during my eighth-grade year at Holy Spirit," said Bierck. "I went on to win on the regional level at Little

Flower, and then it was on to Butler University for the state finals with schools from all over the area. I won an honorable mention at that event."

Lacking a big win at the state competition, Bierck still made a splash for his entry when he was featured in an *Indianapolis News* story about the science fair. "As I recall, I was used in the paper because I was the only kid in the area who was wearing a sport coat, not because of my exhibit," he mused. "However, the inclusion of science fairs shows that CYO, at the time, was not only about sports, but was also for other kids who were maybe not so good at sports, but who were more academic."

Today the CYO Science Fair accommodates up to eight entries from each of the deanery schools throughout Indianapolis. Exhibits are more elaborate and include intense study coupled with experimentation in life and physical sciences, such as a dog's sense of color, the effects of rust on steel wool and whether bigger is really better.

Greg Bierck's awards from the CYO Science Fair in 1967. His exhibit on paleontology garnered him a photo in the *Indianapolis News* the same year. *Awards courtesy of Greg Bierck.*

Karne Cadnix and Leslie Roberts of St. Joseph pose for a shot with their display on crystals, which won them trophies during the 1968 CYO Science Fair. *Courtesy of Indianapolis CYO.*

"I did a project on the solar system, but it was never as sophisticated as this kind of thing, and I never advanced all the way to the city fair at the CYO Center," said Brian Fillenwarth, a former St. Lawrence parishioner who watched his son, Joe, who attended Christ the King School, receive an Outstanding Exhibitor Award at the citywide fair.

"It's not as big of an event as it used to be," said Ed Tinder. "It's not always required at schools anymore, and many teachers have so much material to cover in the school year that they don't have time to have science fairs, but we think it is important, and we want to encourage kids to participate in the science fair. I am always amazed at the ideas they come up with."

CHAPTER 8

Growing, Leading and Serving

I can't imagine a greater cause in which to be engaged.
—President John F. Kennedy

The CYO consistently expanded its programming whenever there was a need and believed that children should be encouraged to socialize and serve their parishes in their own special way. Until the mid-1950s, few outlets actually catered to the youth sandwiched between childhood and adulthood with their own taste in music, movies, clothes and diversions. There was still some fear that idle minds and hands would spell trouble if not occupied in a constructive manner, but with CYO, there was an organization providing safe and supervised programs catering to the needs of teens and tweens.

CYO board members and organizers also knew that the more active a child was in their parish, the more likely they would remain active throughout adulthood. Helping these young people foster healthy relationships, leadership and service opportunities all but guaranteed an active and thriving parish community.

Crossing the Border

The ability to intermingle with the opposite gender is something many of today's middle school students take for granted. There was a time when playgrounds and classrooms were segregated between boys and girls, with designated guards patrolling the boundary lines in order to ensure that no unnecessary conversation took place.

"We called it 'No Man's Land,'" said Steve Warren, noting that CYO activities such as dance parties, picnics and informal get-togethers somewhat diffused the mysteries surrounding the opposite sex. "It [CYO] helped us interact with each other at a time when it was a little awkward."

As a young girl, Terry Williams used to walk home from school with her brothers and their buddies, never finding it at all strange to be close to the opposite gender. The conservative priest at her parish disagreed, however, and became concerned that she was "boy crazy." When a CYO chapter was finally instituted at the northside parish, she said that her parents were thrilled that their kids had a place to hang out with others on a Sunday night and felt good that these programs gave children the chance to socialize with one another.

"We did so many neat things," she said. "It wasn't like we sat around acting all holy or anything. We didn't do Bible readings, but we might have

The 1970 publications team was just one of the kinds of activities that brought young men and women together in a way that enabled them to network with one another. *Courtesy of Indianapolis CYO.*

all met for Mass prior to the meetings. It was just more of an opportunity for us to have somewhere to go and something to do on a Sunday night at a time when few of us had cars, and fewer still had a lot of spending money."

Ed Fillenwarth Jr. said that the success of a parish CYO chapter was largely dependent on the support given to it by the priests, in addition to the head of the group, who had to bond with the children and encourage them to get involved. "Without question, if the kids bonded with the leader, a parish would have a strong CYO program," he said. "In order to have the prosperous program, kids had to have someone that was friendly, who was interested in the people they were working with and who connected with them."

Warren said that other than a priest acting as a moderator and offering the opening and closing prayer, one wouldn't have gathered that it was a religious event at all, and yet whether they were merely informal groups or full-fledged chapters with officers and agendas, the CYO Cadet and Junior programs helped enhance parish identity and everyone from the pastor to the parents were supportive of that.

St. Christopher earns the title CYO Chapter of the Year in 1960 and was presented with its award at the annual CYO banquet. *Courtesy of Indianapolis CYO.*

CYO programs enabled young people to establish a solid and autonomous identity within their parishes and feel confident that their voices were heard. The archdiocese understood that active young people became active adults, and it felt that it was important to stress to these kids that they were a vital part of the community.

"We Expect Something of You"

From these groups on the parish level came the Deanery Youth Councils, which were formed to create an atmosphere of growth and development for all Junior CYO members of the deanery by identifying and developing activities that would engage kids and keep them active in the CYO, as well as to encourage participation in the projects and contests of the National CYO Federation and the archdiocesan CYO. Attendance at the National CYO Convention was encouraged, along with providing representation to the Archdiocesan Youth Council, which was established in 1950 as a means of providing for an exchange of program ideas among the deaneries, as well as offering an adult moderator to meet with officers and provide them with any guidance and advice that they might need to execute their jobs to the best of their ability. In 1951, a delegation from this group represented the archdiocese on the state level, as well as at the National CYO Convention in Cincinnati.

Kathy Schopper attended St. Catherine's School for her elementary education and then went on to St. Mary's Academy. Like others in the 1960s, the CYO was a big part of her life, and she was eager to take part in the variety shows and other social events around the city with her friends. She said that the CYO was her social life and part of her overall high school experience. "Priests were around, but it was more or less a social group," she said. "It was such a shame that my kids didn't have CYO in the same way that I did. We had some great experiences in CYO."

In 1963, Schopper saved the money that she made from babysitting and working a part-time job at the local library in order to attend the CYO National Convention in New York City. She rode to New York in a bus with other members and good-natured chaperones and then stayed at the Hilton Hotel across the street from Radio City Music Hall.

"Those conventions could get wild, even though we did have chaperones," Schopper said. "There were some kids who came back and were kicked out of their chapters for their behavior. Now I never did anything like that, of course, but there were some who did."

Schopper and the other convention attendees had the shock of their young lives when an unexpected guest speaker arrived on November 15: President John F. Kennedy. He was in town on a goodwill mission to speak before a gathering of the American Federation of Labor and Congress of Industrial Organizations (AFL-CIO) but popped into the CYO convention to address the assembly.

"It wasn't scheduled and it was completely unannounced, but we all crowded into the ballroom to see him," Schopper said, reflecting on that moment in history. "We only knew about it through word of mouth. Someone said, 'Kennedy's here,' and we all went to see him. I caught a glimpse of him from a distance, but I couldn't see too well because I was only four-eleven."

The president was not the only member of the Kennedy clan who attended CYO events. Over the years, Robert "Bobby" Kennedy was spotted at several CYO breakfasts and conventions around the country, while little brother Edward "Ted" Kennedy often stumped for his brothers at CYO picnics in the New England area. He even made an appearance at Scecina Memorial High School along with Bobby's wife, Ethel, during Bobby's presidential campaign in 1968. The famous political family always encouraged the youth of America to become socially aware and to find ways in which they could serve.

As for his appearance at the CYO convention, President Kennedy delivered an impassioned five-minute speech to his "fellow members of the CYO" on "Youth in Service" (the theme of the convention) by telling them that each of them were called to serve their families, their churches and their country and to give the best of their talents in all stages of their lives:

> *I realize this meeting is not only a meeting of the youth of today, but those of whom we expect so much in the future. Winston Churchill once said that democracy is the worst form of government except for all of the other systems that have been tried. It is the most difficult, it requires more of you: discipline, character, self-restraint, a willingness to serve the public interest as well as our own private interests. All of these priests, and sisters who have gathered you from all over the United States don't do it because they want you to do well…it is because they regard you as the future leaders of the United States, as future leaders of a great free country. That's why I come here today, not just because you are doing well or because you are outstanding students, but because we expect something of you…*
>
> *I hope that you will spend your time well now and I hope that in a long life, you will recognize your obligations to the Great Republic and to those*

> *who need your help. To help those millions of boys and girls who drop out of school, who can't find work, who live in underprivileged areas…they look to you and they look to me to serve, so I hope you will serve. Serve not only your families and your churches, but serve your country. It deserves the best. It has been generous to us all and we must be generous in return. I congratulate you all on what you have done, and most of all I congratulate you on what you are going to do.*

"Exactly one week later, he was assassinated," Schopper said.

REPRESENTING THE MASSES

Kennedy's legacy to young people to serve in whatever capacity they could was something that CYO members continued to heed long after he was cut down in his prime. Though they were not old enough to join the thousands in the Peace Corps, they still strove to earn their money, pay their dues and serve as delegates to the National Convention each year, where there were opportunities to network with one another and discuss concepts and ideas that were important to the younger generation.

Terry Williams recalled the fun and excitement of serving as a local officer and delegate to the CYO conventions. Local families opened up their homes to visiting youngsters, an action that often planted the seeds for lifelong friendships. During the event, Williams said that she attended meetings and breakout sessions of interest, while meeting other CYO representatives from all over the country. "The topics in our sessions were never heavy, of course, but they were pertinent to our age group," she said. "There was also a dance and a banquet, which was very exciting."

The National CYO Convention was created to promote unity, Christian witness and leadership among the Catholic youth of the United States, according to the CYO handbook. It would provide a focused, educational, liturgical and social experience that strengthened the ministry of Catholic youth.

The National CYO Conventions were able to draw a number of authorities to speak to the delegates on issues that mattered to young people. They put on demonstrations of Catholic faith and celebrated Mass with the thousands in attendance, along with participating in small group panel sessions in which every facet of the organization and its programs were discussed.

A big focus of the convention was the election of the national youth officers of the federation who would help establish program and policy directions for the national CYO Federation. Williams said that she remembered plenty of politicking and good-natured campaigning going on among the hopeful candidates during the event, but it was always in the spirit of fun.

"I went to Miami, Florida, to the convention when I was sixteen," she said. "We stayed at the Fontainebleau Hotel during the event, and we were running Dave Schneider for office. There was a plane load of us who went, along with several priests and chaperones, of course."

Because Williams was an officer, her trip was subsidized, but she said that everyone who went worked together in order to split the costs: "When I was a freshman in college, they all rallied behind me as I ran for national vice-president of the CYO in Denver. I was elected, and it was great to work behind the scenes of the organization and meet people from all over. They were all such dear people."

The CYO convention segued into the National Catholic Youth Conference (NCYC) in 1983. The conference is now a three-day biennial event held in cities all over the country, including Indianapolis, which held its first NCYC in 1991. The conference was partially underwritten via a grant from the Lilly Endowment, Inc., and was enjoyed by local Catholic youths, as well as visiting CYOers from all parts of the nation. In 2011, the Circle City once again played host to the NCYC, with the theme "Called to Glory."

World Youth Day

Conferences are not the only way that the Catholic youth of today continue to make their voices heard on a large scale. Pope John Paul II's love for the youth and respect for their unique offering to the Church was something that he championed in a variety of ways. During his first visit to the United States after his election, he told his "Dear Young Friends" everywhere: "You are ready for what Christ wants of you now. He wants you—all of you—to be the light of the world as only young people can be light. It is time to let your light shine!" according to John Vitek.

In 1984, Pope John Paul II invited 300,000 young people to St. Peter's Square on Palm Sunday for the International Jubilee of Youth. Seeing the enthusiastic assembly, the pope said, "Who claimed that today's youth has lost their senses of values?" He then gave the youth the symbol of the love of Christ for humanity known as the "World Youth Day Cross."

Two years later, the pontiff established the first official World Youth Day and planned a massive Palm Sunday celebration in 1986. Since that time, Pope John Paul II and his successor, Pope Benedict XVI, have met with the youth in this gathering to celebrate Mass and remind them of the important role that they play in the church.

"When, back in 1985, I wanted to start the World Youth Days…I imagined a powerful moment in which the young people of the world could meet Christ, who is eternally young, and could learn from him how to be bearers of the gospel to other young people…millions have taken part and, as a result, have become better and more committed Christian witnesses," said Pope John Paul II at the last World Youth Day he attended before his death in 2005.

Each year, youths and adults from around the diocese make pilgrimages to World Youth Day and other papal appearances, often accompanied by Archbishop Daniel M. Buechlein. "[We] have some wonderful experiences and we see wonderful places, but first and foremost, we are on a pilgrimage," the archbishop said before World Youth Day in 2005. "A pilgrimage differs from other kinds of journeys or trips in that we travel together with a common faith, a common hope, and a common love," he noted, according to Brandon Evans.

Area youths also convene in Washington, D.C., each year, along with other concerned young Catholics, to support the Right to Life March. The march began in 1974 with about 20,000 participants, but in recent years, as many as 200,000 people have come out to show their support for the movement, and a significant number of them have been young people involved with CYO and youth ministry activities in their individual parishes.

Susan Goley, of Madison, participated in a recent Right to Life March and said that the right to life from the moment of conception is something that she prays about and is willing to stand up for. As the junior at Shawe Memorial Jr./Sr. High School said, it has always been important for her to eschew the media images of acceptable moral behavior in favor of a more faith-based path. She was quick to point out in an interview with the *Criterion*, the local weekly Catholic newspaper, that her parents have raised her as a Catholic and that if she can be a proponent for the pro-life movement, even as a student, she was willing to do so. "I think about what God and my parents would want from me," she said, according to Wyand.

David Leszcynski, a student at Marian University, is an example of a young person whose ties to his faith community have evolved as he has grown. From participating in youth choir in grade school and remaining an active member of his parish throughout high school, despite his many commitments, he has attended the National Catholic Youth Conference, Right to Life Marches and even saw Pope Benedict XVI when he was in the United States for a visit in 2008.

"I didn't even know I was going until it was the last day to sign up," he said. "It was an incredible experience to see the leader of the worldwide church. To have a visible leader that I know took his faith and vocation seriously was truly inspiring." His experiences afford him the opportunity to mentor young Catholics during their Christian Awakening Retreats in their senior year of high school. Leszcynski said that he remembered how important his own retreat was and that he feels called to bring that same feeling into the life of other young people on the precipice of adulthood: "It was a moment truly given to me by Christ and filled with the Holy Spirit to evaluate where I was going with my life. That's why I go back and lead when I can. The youth are the leaders of tomorrow, and if I can bring Christ into a single youth's life, then I know I am doing what God wants me to do."

CHAPTER 9
SENIOR CYO

Bless our friendship before marriage.

—Catholic prayer

Young adult Catholics, just beyond their senior year of high school, find themselves at an emotional crossroads in their lives after the excitement of graduation wears off. Some know that the next step in their lives will be college or vocational schools, while others may join the armed forces or work in the private sector, but in the 1950s and 1960s, young adults were at a loss for parochial involvement and desperate for the connection they once had through CYO activities. It was easy to feel lost in the shuffle once you were beyond the age of an altar server but not quite ready for the altar yourself.

It's a concept that is as relevant today as it was when Indianapolis was decades away from becoming the thriving metropolis it is today. Though there were amenities in the Circle City—such as the Indiana Fairgrounds Coliseum, Hinkle Fieldhouse and Clowes Hall—those activities cost gas and money and were not always available to young people on a budget.

Having come of age at a time when society finally began to recognize that adolescents had specific needs and interests, and after helping to pioneer a new age of music, clothing and independence, these post–high school young adults continued to look for their niche beyond their parents' world. The answer appeared to be to create a faith-based group that could merge friends, fun and fellowship. Senior CYO proved to be the answer to this prayer.

Senior CYO was unique in that it fell under the CYO banner but was recognized as an autonomous entity designed to help young adults remain

Senior CYO events in the early years were often geared to see off soldiers heading to the European and Pacific theaters. Designed for the post–high school set, Senior CYO encouraged wholesome coed mingling. *Courtesy of Indianapolis CYO.*

connected to their parishes and the Catholic community, while developing a deeper relationship with their peer group. Senior CYO recognized the unique social needs of the "out of high school but not yet married" demographic and was committed to offering a variety of social opportunities that brought like-minded people together.

What started with a golf outing in the early years of this CYO program grew to encompass a wide range of offerings; Senior CYO gave post-adolescents the chance to meet new people and strengthen old friendships with classmates who were also facing the real world for the very first time.

A Social Network

Before Facebook, MySpace and Twitter gave everyone the chance to connect and update one another with life-altering news, young people had to congregate in order to catch up on one another's "status." What better way than through the CYO?

Though it has been part of the CYO program from the outset, Senior CYO has been one of the more challenging CYO branches to maintain. The war years took their toll on the membership. As men flocked to the military, there was certainly an impact on the number (and gender) of participants. Women, too, were very busy with their contributions to the war effort, selling war bonds, collecting scrap material and planting victory gardens, but there wasn't always a lot of time to be more involved when they often took on more of the responsibility in the home, and their mothers went to work. CYO dances were very popular places to find young adults, but a solid membership was often hard to maintain.

The archdiocese hoped that each Senior CYO chapter would be a unit that took part in a balanced program of spiritual, social, cultural and athletic activities similar to its junior counterpart. However, for a variety of reasons, Senior CYO struggled in the postwar era, and many parochial chapters simply died out.

Throughout the 1950s and '60s, the archdiocese made a concerted effort to rebuild and revive the Senior CYO program, wanting to return it to "a strength and status comparable to that first decade of the Indianapolis CYO," according to the 1964 twenty-fifth anniversary annual report.

Ed Trumpey was typical of the sort of young adult who needed Senior CYO in his life. Trumpey said that he participated sporadically in junior CYO events at St. Francis de Sales Parish on the city's eastside (today home to Martin University in the Brightwood neighborhood) before graduating from Scecina Memorial High School. He said that the gatherings were loosely organized and little more than drop-ins held in the church basement, where teens practiced the latest dance steps to recordings of big band greats such as Tommy Dorsey, Glen Miller and other super groups of the swing era.

After high school, a traditional college education wasn't economically feasible for Trumpey. Instead he chose to attend Purdue extension classes in the basement of the athletic club in downtown Indianapolis. "It was a God-awful place. I went to school in the dark and came home in the dark. There was no social life there at all," he said.

Those who went to college were at least able to socialize with study groups, pledge fraternity or sorority organizations or become involved with student life activities geared to their particular interests, but Trumpey and others like him who stayed at home were floundering. He turned to his local Senior CYO group for companionship but was disappointed to learn that the chapter was fairly inactive.

Rather than look elsewhere for a social outlet, Trumpey decided to help reorganize the eastside program so that it offered at least one activity a week to help get the group off the ground. He became president of the chapter and began planning events, many of which started out as dance parties in someone's home, a fun yet economical activity. As interest in the group grew, members began forming committees to help plan social, athletic and cultural events based on members' individual interests. Trumpey said that in time, as the group expanded, members could be busy every night of the week. "There was always something going on," he said.

The activities could literally be anything. Card parties, picnics, bowling, potluck suppers, day trips, dance classes at the Jewish Community Center and camping overnighters were all part of the Senior CYO fun. Unlike other CYO groups, Senior CYO had the luxury of being able to plan activities based on the membership's interest, and while some of them were held in the parish basements and recreation rooms, others were held offsite. There were no limits to what the groups might engage in on any given weekend.

Trumpey said that there were some members who were interested in exploring the wild caves of the area and invested in miner's hats and lanterns for spelunking expeditions. The rest of the group accompanied the explorers and set up a picnic lunch in a cave as part of their contribution to the outing, while the cave divers sloshed through the muck and mud, often crawling on their stomachs to get through the tighter spots. "Somewhere I know there is a picture of them all covered in mud up to their necks," Trumpey said with a laugh.

"I remember when Ed got stuck in the cave, and none of us could get past him," said Gerry Kramer, another member of St. Francis de Sales, who joined the Senior CYO group after returning from his service in the navy. He said that he liked the Senior CYOers because they offered him companionship and camaraderie. "We did plays and had a lot of cookouts. It was a great experience for young people."

Other activities were more athletic in nature. With discretionary income at a minimum, local parks became Sunday afternoon stomping grounds for picnics and sporting events. Senior CYO members said that the group might arrange a pickup game of volleyball or softball, while others lolled on the grass and talked.

"We even had these road derbies, which were scavenger hunts on wheels and progressive dinners," said Loretta (Dalton) Miller, a former Our Lady of Lourdes parishioner and member of the Eastside Senior CYO. "We would drive from one place to the next all over the city and have appetizers at one place, the main course at the next and dessert at someone else's house."

Ed Chesterson said that he loved the Senior CYO group and especially enjoyed the meetings that were held in the basement of St. Philip Neri's, where there was a working four-lane bowling alley. The facility led to the beginnings of the bowling league, which sported many members from the eastside group, as well as other Senior CYO chapters around the city. Eventually, the growth in the bowling league's popularity caused its members to relocate to Miracle Lanes. Julian Wagner, who became affiliated with the group while on hiatus from Butler University, said that Senior CYO was a great place to meet people who were like-minded and willing to have some fun. He socialized not only with the members of the eastside group but also with the group that met at Cathedral High School, taking in trips to Pokagon State Park and long weekends down at Camp Rancho.

"The girls would stay in one cabin and the guys would be in the other," he recalled. "We were all in our twenties so there weren't any chaperones, but we were all pretty well behaved. It also helped that we all shared the same belief system and were of the same faith."

The Eastside Senior CYO group on a trip to Pokagon State Park. Weekend trips were a big part of the program and included trips to South Bend and Camp Rancho, as well as exploring in wild caves of the area. *Courtesy of Loretta Miller.*

Dances were always popular events, and the Senior CYO groups often pooled their resources in order to use a K of C hall and hire a live band for the evening or partnered with other Christian groups. The organizing committee would select a theme for the evening. One memorable dance concerned a Halloween bash that saw several members in creative costumes such as "Adam and Eve in Pair-o-Dice" (complete with dotted white boxes to represent game cubes). Patty Murphy borrowed fellow member George McMullin's marine dress blue uniform, tucked her ponytail into her hat and wore a mask, fooling everyone in attendance. No one could guess her true identity. "They all thought I was Gene Bowman," she laughed, remembering what a good time those fall dances provided for the group. "They were always crowded."

The Common Denominator

Though they didn't bang the drum or quote scripture and verse at every opportunity, faith was indeed a core component of Senior CYO. Trumpey said that the groups received a lot of support from the clergy of the area, who were only too willing to donate meeting space, help young people socialize, encourage new members and do whatever it took to grow the organization. Trumpey said that Senior CYO became so successful that finding a meeting space that could hold everyone became a problem. "Luckily, Father Ed Sorgel at Little Flower was very welcoming to us. We also joined with another Senior CYO group from the westside, and that just made us even bigger."

Jack Mears was a member of the Westside Senior CYO League who found his way over to the eastside group when membership dwindled at St. Anthony's. Mears was encouraged to join Senior CYO by his sister, who was a student at Marian College (now Marian University). He agreed but noticed that the numbers had dropped since his sister had been active, and he began looking for a new group to join. He called the CYO office and obtained a list of available programs, and after visiting them all, he said that he clicked with the eastside group and became a very active member. "They even elected me president a couple of times," he said. "One of my goals was to visit the high schools and try to help the seniors become involved in Senior CYO after graduation. We didn't want them falling through the cracks."

For members, the Senior CYO experience became a way to practice their faith outside of school and away from parents but within a supportive atmosphere. On occasion, members would meet in a local tavern, such as McShane's Lounge. Trumpey said that alcohol wasn't a big part of the program, even though most were of legal drinking age. "Even at house parties, it just wasn't part of what we did," he said.

The young adults also made Mass attendance a group affair, rising early to fulfill their obligation before going out to breakfast, either at someone's home or a local establishment such as Harold's Steer-In, then heading to Brookside Park to while away the afternoon. The faith component served as an underlying foundation for what was a social network of friends.

"The after-Mass parties at Bill Shaver's house were the best," said Miller, who agreed that faith, as well as fun, served as the common denominator for Senior CYO members. Shaver was very involved in the Catholic community at Butler University through Newman House and said it offered him a great

The Eastside Senior CYO group at a party after Mass at a member's home. The group was a wonderful way for young people of like-minded faith to fellowship with one another. *Courtesy of Loretta Miller.*

opportunity to stay connected with other single post–high school adults, but Senior CYO also offered something more. He said that it kept him connected to his parish family and helped him develop friendships that underscored his faith.

Officers were sworn in and given a blessing during Mass at the beginning of their tenure, and the group made a point of engaging in service work through local social agencies in order to do things to give back to the community.

"We would go to church together once a month; we would also have Father come to our meetings and offer a homily or a talk on things that were happening in the community," Miller said. "We would also attend Stations and Benediction during Lent before going to someone's house and partying for a while. It was really neat."

He said that his parents were welcoming of the group using their home as a hangout and that they considered many of the guys as surrogate sons; there were also a fair number of non-Catholics who were part of the group, as well, and they were also welcomed as members of the family.

New Members and Ideas Were Welcome

The group also considered service to be a part of the overall mission of the program, and members constantly looked for ways to make an impact on the community. For several years, Senior CYO members put together plays, musicals and other entertainment programs to raise money for local organizations or to donate food baskets to the poor.

"Carol Foxen was a dance instructor, and we would put together a minstrel show at Scecina, back when you could still do something like that, and we sold quite a few tickets," said Trumpey. "Jack Mears was involved in that as well, I believe, and anything we made from it was donated. It was not a commercial venture for us. It seems we did that for about two or three years. We even had a musical and entertained down at St. Paul's Hermitage."

After relocating to Indianapolis with her parents in 1957, Carol (Foxen) Ley said that she only had about a week to settle in before beginning her sophomore year at Scecina High School. As the oldest of six children, Ley spent a good portion of her high school years helping to take care of her siblings, leaving little time to socialize with school chums. She graduated in 1960 and began taking dance classes at the Jordan School of Music.

The Senior CYO group performing at the St. Paul Hermitage. The group often put on musical revues and shows to raise money for service projects. *Courtesy of Loretta Miller.*

"I also worked," she said. "My parents were big on us working when we were out of school, but they were also eager for me to get out and meet people, so even though we went to St. Bernadette's, they drove me over to Little Flower where the Senior CYO group was meeting."

Ley said that she found a wonderful peer group that gave those who weren't away at school a network of people with whom they could socialize. Once the meeting portion was over, the members would sit around and play cards, those of legal age might go get a drink and others would head over to Brody's for a snack.

As for the talent showcases and shows, Ley said that during parties and other get-togethers, talents emerged. "We would notice that someone might be good at telling jokes or that someone could sing well," she said. "After a while, everyone encouraged each other, and along with some practices, the shows came off really well."

Meet Your Mate

Senior CYO offered not only opportunity for friendship and fun but also the chance to meet a Catholic soul mate with whom you could share your life. Below the surface of the primary functions of Senior CYO, one cannot help but notice the amount of marriages that came out of the group in the days before Match.com, eHarmony and other services dominated the singles market. In fact, there was such a high ratio of marriages that occurred via Senior CYO that the group ran out of wedding present ideas. "We finally settled on a white Bible with their name engraved on it," said Trumpey.

In the 1950s and '60s, gender roles were clearly defined, and it was generally accepted that there were two paths one could follow: the call to a religious vocation or the call to married life. There wasn't a lot of middle ground. As for the latter, women were expected to be the nurturing wife and mother without having to work outside the home. A man was to be the provider by holding a good job and remain an upstanding citizen in the parish, as well as the community.

Getting there required some restrained social time with the opposite sex. Though the reigning rules of the day may seem a little contrived by today's standards, it is safe to say that dating practices were less complicated then—a lady never asked a gentleman out. When a date was suggested, it was understood that the gentleman would pay for everything. (Keep in mind that few women worked or had spending money of their own.) In addition, she lived at home or with a roommate, which offered some clear parameters as to what time she should arrive back after an evening out, and these arrangements put the kibosh on any sort of coed sleepover.

There was also no confusion about what an evening meant. A date at the time was simply that, a date. An evening out was not a precursor to an exclusive, long-term relationship. People dated around and in groups before considering marriage, and for the most part, until a ring was exchanged, it was assumed that everyone was a free agent.

At the time, the average age of marriage was twenty-two for males and twenty for females, making those Senior CYO years the prime time to find a special guy or gal and plan your life accordingly. Many did just that. The Senior CYO program was a perfect place to find eligible bachelors and bachelorettes. People were less busy than they are today, so there was more of an opportunity for spontaneous socialization. Church socials and dances also encouraged singles to mix, and Senior CYO was no exception.

The Senior CYO groups were a great way to get eligible young men and women together who were looking to meet their mate and settle down. *Courtesy of Indianapolis CYO.*

Savvy male officers knew that the promise of a romance could be a great marketing tool for the organization, not to mention a way to have first dibs on visiting females. According to Murphy, Trumpey and fellow Eastside CYO group member Bill Schopper were known for personally welcoming new women to the group by inviting them on a double date in hopes that they would tell their friends that Senior CYO was a great place to meet men and would stick around to become active members (a ploy that usually worked!). "I think they dated every girl in the program at one time or another," she said, noting that both ended up meeting their wives through Senior CYO.

"When Bill got married, we were all in the wedding party, and he had these new shoes on. During the ceremony, when he had to kneel at the altar, we saw that he had written 'Goodbye girls!' on his shoes," Trumpey laughed.

Kathy Schopper, Bill's widow, met her husband not through Senior CYO but rather the Young Catholic Adults organization, a similar social group for Catholic singles. Bill was ten years older than her and had been engaged twice before finally reaching the altar.

"I joined YCA in 1971 out of desperation for a social group where I could meet nice people and have a crowd to run around with. By the time I met Bill, the Senior CYO had kind of folded or wasn't very active. I guess joining clubs wasn't very popular. I do know he dated quite a few of the Senior CYO members," she said with a laugh. "At our wedding reception, it was more like 'Who didn't you date?'"

While some officers dated freely, others did not. Mears said that he had a strict policy not to date while in office. "I just didn't feel it was right," he said. "It wasn't for me, but I still met my wife through the group."

Ley didn't meet her husband through Senior CYO but said that because she was a little younger than some of the other members, when she did date, her CYO "big brothers" were quick to give their opinions of the guys she socialized with. "It was a nice feeling that they were looking out for me," she said. "In the end, I was only active in Senior CYO for about three or four years before I married and moved to Ohio, but my sister was in it after me. Dating wasn't the purpose of the group, but it just happened. People would

Weddings among Senior CYO members, such as Maryann and Ed Chesterson, were common, and many of the members say that they met their mates through the group. *Courtesy of Our Lady of Lourdes.*

get together as a group and then get to know each other and pair off. They were all such a great group of people, and I have so many find memories of that group."

Maryann Chesterson was a secretary at Our Lady of Lourdes in Irvington and was told by one of the clergy members that she needed to get involved in Senior CYO or he would drag her to a meeting himself. She suspected that he was hoping she would meet a good Catholic boy to date. Just recently, she and her husband, Ed, whom she did meet in the program, celebrated their golden anniversary. "At least 90 percent of our group met their spouses at CYO. I think what helped is that it was so localized, and we had the chance to do so much together."

MURPHY'S ROMANCE

Forget Ryan O'Neal and Allie McGraw, real-life love stories abound in Senior CYO, though none quite as touching as the twice-in-a-lifetime experience that happened to Pat Hibbert-Murphy that can only be described as extraordinary.

Murphy was from St. Philip Neri Parish and was a shy girl who joined the group as a way to get to know the people with whom she'd attended high school on a completely different and deeper level before settling down into marriage. She could not have imagined that she would meet both of her husbands through the program.

It was something out of a cheesy teen romance novel the day that she received two marriage proposals from the men she had been dating in the organization. "I didn't know what to do, so I ended up calling my sister and hanging out with her [to sort it out]. We ended up at a retreat where the name 'John' kept coming up [the name of one of her suitors]. I took it as a sign," she said, noting that the couple was together twenty years before their marriage ended.

A few years after her divorce, Murphy received a call from Bill Murphy, whom she still kept in touch with through yearly Senior CYO reunion events. He mentioned that he, too, was going through a divorce, and after that was finalized, they started seeing each other socially and finally began dating again. "However, I made him wait two years before marrying!" She said with a laugh. "It is funny how things worked out, but Senior CYO was definitely a tremendous opportunity to meet people and marry someone with the same religious values."

Growing Pains

Cathy Heitman Mears, a Scecina High School graduate who married Jack Mears, said that in some ways, the group's ability to make matches among its members might have worked a little too well. "I do think that's what killed the Senior CYO programs. Everyone paired up, got married and started their lives. The last Senior CYO event we went to, there was only a handful of people there."

"People went through at different times, and then eventually everyone got married, and the whole thing disappeared," said Trumpey, noting that he wanted his daughter to experience the same level of camaraderie that he had in CYO. He tried to start a group at St. Luke's on the northside, but without a lot of active members to keep it going, plus everyone's busy schedule, it is hard to maintain. "I always thought there should be another Senior CYO, though."

"I really think that the era of the Senior CYO has passed," said Kramer. "It was nice, but kids today don't find clubs popular, and they don't like to join things. It's tough, though, because I think it's sad that we don't have a lot of young people just out of high school staying as connected with the church like we used to."

Senior CYO may no longer exist in a traditional sense, but the spirit of the group still lingers on in various incarnations geared to meet the needs of young adult Catholics through organizations that continue to try and give people a chance to remain connected to their faith community. A number of colleges and universities in the Central Indiana area have established programs to offer faith formation, as well as a social outlet in the same vein that the Senior CYO had in decades past. The Young Adult Catholics (YCA) have established chapters through Newman Centers at a variety of schools. There are multiple opportunities for Catholics to fellowship with one another. Spirit & Truth also enables young people to gather in prayer before meeting at a local restaurant for a bite to eat.

Shaver said that he has seen some progress in moving toward a new, updated version of Senior CYO that has taken off at Holy Spirit Catholic Church on the city's eastside. While they do not call it CYO, the youth ministry coordinator has made a commitment to keep kids involved in parish life.

"It's got a lot of the same principles that we have of getting together, having a faith component and still socializing with one another through skating or going out to eat. Man, I sure remember the times we would go

A Senior CYO reunion picture taken at Fort Harrison State Park. Members gather once a year to rekindle friendships and remember the good old days of Senior CYO. *Courtesy of George McMullin.*

out to eat, and we would be there two hours just hanging out and having a good time. I hope they get the same kind of enjoyment out of it that we did," said Shaver.

Perhaps these groups will carry the spirit of Senior CYO forward for the next generation in a city that has expanded and grown rapidly in the decades since Trumpey and the others first gathered together in a basement and decided to make their own place in their parish and the larger Catholic community.

"I wish there was another Senior CYO," said Miller. "I would like to see a group like that in which my own college daughter could participate."

CONCLUSION

THE FUTURE OF CYO

The one human hope of the modern world is youth.
—Bishop Bernard J. Sheil

Visionaries and innovators are often unaware of the impact their ideas have on modern society. Johann Gutenberg could not have imagined a day when his movable type would not only be the catalyst for mass-produced Bibles but also influence everything from typewriters to word processors, computers and even the techno-touch wonders of the twenty-first century. It's hard to see Alexander Graham Bell envisioning the simple telephone as a unit on which people would talk, text, surf the Internet and watch movies, all with a tap of a screen. Who knows if Henry Ford had the foresight to see how robotic technology would one day change the way we operate assembly lines?

However, those who pioneer groundbreaking initiatives for youth tend to fall into a different category. They tend to see the need for the constant evolution of their ideas and realize that the only way to have that eternal appeal is to remain current with the times and to constantly involve forward-thinking leaders who understand the possibilities for future advancement.

Bishop Bernard J. Sheil saw the CYO program for exactly what it could become: a living, breathing part of the Catholic Church that would grow and change with the generations. He worked tirelessly to achieve it, and so did everyone else who brought Sheil's vision to fruition in cities all around the country.

"No project has ever been completely installed and running smoothly before the next is on the production line, with Bishop Sheil driving immediate action," wrote Treat. "Outsiders have watched him, too, and whatever apprehension they may have felt soon turned to admiration."

In the 1930s, the Catholic Youth Organization was nothing more than a way to keep kids off the street. It was a male-dominated boxing club that segued into a social and educational organization with a faith component. As it grew and moved into other cities throughout the 1940s, it became an outlet for young people, as well as a way for them to connect to their parish through athletic programs, summer camps, cultural opportunities and social get-togethers that would encourage them to become lifelong members of their local Catholic community.

The movement exploded locally in the 1950s and '60s, with numerous activities for young people, and then it fell on hard times in the '70s and '80s as the youth ministry movement bisected the CYO in many parishes. However, the organization moved on and is always on the lookout for ways to bring programs that matter to the youth of Central Indiana.

A group shot of the CYO Sing-off event at Butler University in the 1960s. *Courtesy of the Indianapolis CYO.*

Kevin Sullivan said that the presence of Camp Rancho Framasa is a wonderful extension of the classroom for teachers who wish to bring their students down for nature studies, for religious groups who use the facility for retreats and for yearlong programming designed to accommodate parochial needs throughout the year.

Ed Tinder has noted that there are more sports offered through the CYO program today than ever before, due to the amount of kids who want to be part of an organized team and know that through CYO everyone has the chance to play and do their best on the field. The music festival includes not only individual performers but also school bands and youth choirs that previously did not exist on the parish level in large numbers. Even the annual science fair has taken on a depth that few could have imagined even thirty years ago. For the current generation, participating in CYO activities is still a relevant part of their lives and a heritage to which they are proud to be connected.

Joe Fillenwarth, of Christ the King parish, is the great-grandson of CYO organizer Ed Fillenwarth Sr. He said that it means a lot to him to be the

Handicrafts at Camp Rancho in the 1970s, where youngsters have come throughout the years to learn and grow. *Courtesy of Camp Rancho Framasa.*

fourth generation of his family connected with the CYO and hopes that one day he will be a coach. "I want to stay involved," he said, shyly. "I will probably be a track or cross country coach."

Joe's father, Brian, said that it's great to see how the CYO has grown over the years. "I am sure that the organizers, such as my grandfather, are looking down on us and are very proud of what the CYO has accomplished in the Indianapolis area, but I am sure it is what they imagined it could be back in 1939."

Ed Fillenwarth Jr. said that when his father and the other organizers of Central Indiana's CYO program first got together in 1939, they wanted a program that would continue to grow and prosper while always keeping the needs of the youth at the forefront of the mission. It is a belief that is as relevant today as it was in the first half of the twentieth century.

"The CYO is constantly looking at their programs and evaluating them to see what should be added, what needs to be dropped or changed," said Fillenwarth Jr. "When you have the wonderful leadership that we have had over the years, including Bill Sahm, Bill Kuntz and Ed Tinder, you have a heck of a start. Who knows where it will go from here?"

APPENDIX
Indianapolis CYO Timeline

1815 John Bosco is born in Piedmont, Italy, on August 16.

1835 Bosco joins the seminary and is ordained a priest six years later.

1842 Bosco begins his first oratory for boys in February.

1888 Bosco dies in January.
Bernard James Sheil is born in Chicago on February 18.

1906 Sheil graduates from St. Viator College in Bourbonnais, Illinois.

1910 Sheil is ordained.

1928 Sheil is named Auxillary Bishop of Chicago.

1930 Sheil establishes the Catholic Youth Organization (CYO), a boxing club for at-risk boys.

1932 Sheil opens first CYO Center in Chicago in June.

1934 Bosco is canonized St. Giovanni (John) Melchior Bosco.

1936 Joseph E. Ritter is named the seventh bishop of Indianapolis diocese on March 24.

Buffet suppers and Sunday socials were a major part of the CYO during the World War II era. *Courtesy of Indianapolis CYO.*

1938 First organizational meeting of the Indianapolis CYO is held on December 12.

1939 Indianapolis CYO is officially formed, with Father Charles Schoettelkotte as director.
Senior CYO Deanery Youth Council is formed.
Parochial athletic opportunities are combined under the CYO umbrella.
First Senior CYO unit is formed.
Boys' Junior CYO softball and basketball leagues begin.
First CYO dance is held in April.
CYO golf tournament is held in July.
Priests' committee is formed.
St. John Bosco is chosen as the patron saint of the CYO.

1940 Father Maurice Dugan is named CYO director.
CYO Bulletin is published.
Cadet kickball begins with rules established by Father Bernard Gerdon.
Father Richard Langdon is named CYO director in September.
The Senior CYO tennis league, Table Tennis Tournament, Basketball League and tournament are held.
Junior CYO holds its first basketball league and begins a table tennis league.

1941 Jack Nelson becomes first Junior Youth Council president.
Seniors hold first one-act play contest.
Ad Altre Dei medal is presented to Catholic Scouts.

1942 Sheil establishes the CYO Educational Department and the Sheil School of Social Studies in Chicago.
Catholic USO is formed due to World War II.
Sunday afternoon socials are held for servicemen.
First Hobby Show is held.
Senior CYO Bowling League is established.

1943 Father Richard Kavanagh is named CYO director.
CYO takes over Catholic Salvage Bureau.

1945 *Youth and Religion* radio program hit the airwaves on WISH.

1946 CYO receives 280 acres of land from Mr. and Mrs. Bert Dingley, to be used as a summer camp.
First camping season at Rancho Framasa is held over the summer.

1947 Land is purchased on the corner of Harding and Sixteenth Streets to be used as an athletic complex for CYO sports.
Archdiocesan basketball tournaments begin.
Camp is extended to four sessions.
Camp fund drive is established.

1949 Construction is completed at athletic complex, and the dedication is held in September.
Inaugural game is played.

After parochial-based programs were merged under the CYO umbrella, golf was one of the first established CYO sports. *Courtesy of Indianapolis CYO.*

1950 First Archdiocesan Youth Council meeting is held.
Board of directors is reactivated.

1951 Junior one-act play contest is held for the first time.
Cadet Hobby Show is started at the Catholic Community Center.
First National Catholic Youth Convention is held in Cincinnati.

1953 Sheil celebrates his twenty-fifth anniversary as auxiliary bishop of Chicago.
Cadet Football Jamboree is held for the first time at the CYO Stadium.

1954 First CYO banquet is held, and first St. John Bosco medals are presented.
Junior Swim meet is held at Broad Ripple pool.
Junior Tennis Tournament is held.
Talent contest is held for the first time in August.
William Sahm is named executive secretary of CYO.

1955 Junior Style Show and Dance gets underway.
Catholic Quiz contest begins in February.
Father John Elford is named CYO director.
Press box is added to CYO Stadium.
Junior CYO Kickball begins.

1956 Christ the King wins "Junior CYO of the Year" award at annual banquet.

1957 Parochial Songfest is held at Butler University for the first time.
Boys' track is added to athletic offerings.
CYO participates in National Adoration Day.

1958 First Archdiocesan CYO convention is held at Marian College in April.
CYO handbook is established.
New CYO office building is constructed adjacent to the stadium.
Marian Medals for Girl Scouts and Junior Catholic Daughters of America are presented.

A flag-raising ceremony at CYO's Camp Rancho Framasa. *Courtesy of Camp Rancho Framasa.*

1959 Girls' track is offered for the first time.
Girls' softball league is established.
Rosary on the Air is broadcast for CYOers on WIRE.
The baking contest is held for the first time.
Adult Advisory Organization takes over from the Adult Counsellor Organization.

1960 Cadet Music Contest is introduced in March.
St. George medal for Boy Scout leaders is presented.
Land for new girls' camp is donated; the proposed name is Camp Christina.

1961 First summer of camp at Camp Christina is offered.
St. Anne Medal for Girl Scout leaders is presented.
Junior Halloween Dance is held.

1962 St. John Bosco Guild is created to help with fundraising and public relations.
The new Monsignor Downey Athletic Field is established on a 13.6-acre tract of land.

1963 Priests' Advisory Board is created.
President John F. Kennedy speaks to members of the CYO at the National Catholic Youth Convention in New York on November 15, 1963.
President Kennedy is assassinated on November 22.

1964 Silver Jubilee of the CYO is held.

1966 Sheil is removed from his position as CYO director-general.

1968 CYO purchases new land for northside athletic field.

1969 Bishop Bernard J. Sheil, the founder of the CYO movement, dies on September 13.

1970 CYO reconsiders its non-Catholic eligibility rule with the help of the Priests' Advisory Committee.

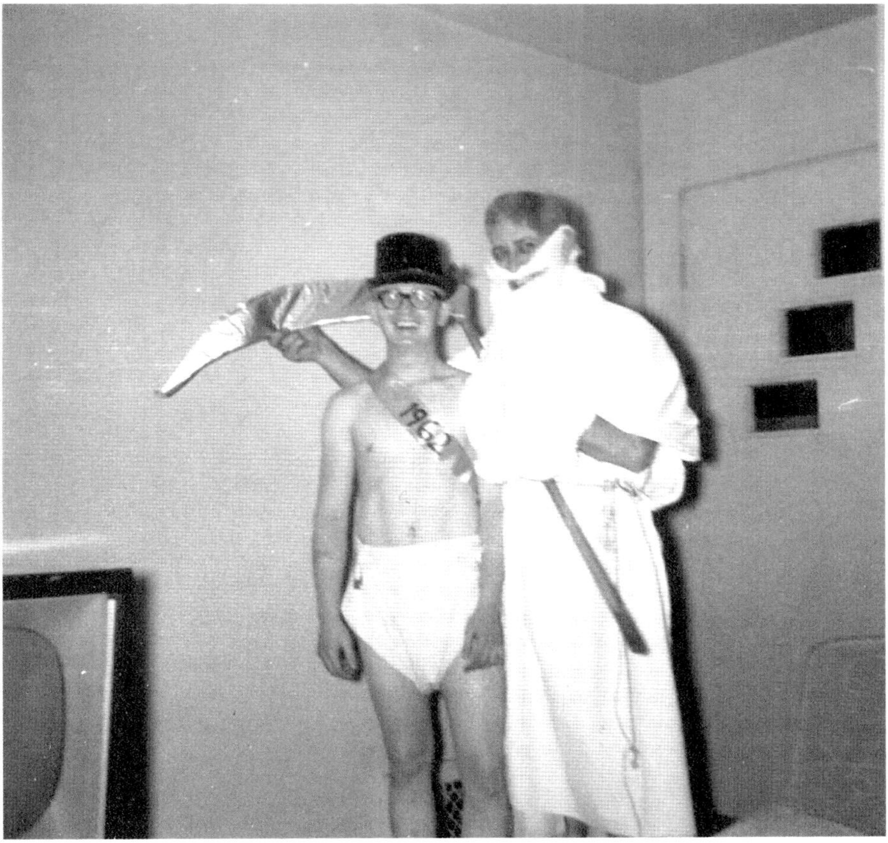

Gene Bowman dresses up as Baby New Year alongside Mr. Henry Foxen's Father Time during a Senior CYO costume party in 1962. *Courtesy of Jim Shaver.*

1971 William Sahm, longtime director of the CYO, dies. He is replaced by Bill Kuntz.

1973 CYO National Convention is held in Indianapolis, with a keynote speech by Danny Thomas.

1974 Camp Rancho Framasa and Camp Christina receive much-needed upgrades thanks to assistance from the Lilly Endowment.

Right to Life March is first held in Washington, D.C., with twenty thousand marchers.

Adult training programs are established for adult volunteers.

A winning farce troupe shows off its prizes after the one-act play contest. *Courtesy of Indianapolis CYO.*

1975 First awards are presented to the outstanding man and female youth leaders in the archdiocese.

1979 CYO Leadership and Service Institute is proposed to certify program volunteers.

1980 Youth ministry programs begin sweeping the nation.
Administrator of teen services is established to develop the new youth ministry program for the archdiocese.

1983 CYO members march in the annual St. Patrick's Day Parade in downtown Indianapolis.

National Youth Conference is held in Washington, D.C., taking over from the CYO Convention.

Members of the Eastside Senior CYO ride in a local parade to encourage new members to join the fun. *Courtesy of Jim Shaver.*

1984 International Jubilee on Youth is held in St. Peter's Square, with Pope John Paul II in attendance.

1985 World Youth Day is instituted.

1989 Alumni are added to the annual talent contest, and they perform a medley from the Broadway show *Grease*.
The Golden Jubilee is held.

1991 National Catholic Youth Conference is held in Indianapolis.

2011 National Catholic Youth Conference, titled "Called to Glory," is held in Indianapolis.

Source: CYO Annual reports and cited websites.

Bibliography

Allenmang, John D., Reverend. "Parents Can Prevent Delinquency." *Our Parish School Bulletin.* Menomonee Falls, WI: Parish Publishers, 1962.

Catholic Diocese of Wilmington. "75 years of CYO Memories." http://www.cdow.org/cyomemories.html.

Catholic Encyclopedia. "St. Giovanni Melchior Bosco." http://www.newadvent.org/cathen/02689d.htm.

Catholic Online. "St. John Bosco." http://www.catholic.org/saints/saint.php?saint_id=63.

Catholic Youth Organization. *50 Years of Golden Memories*. Annual Activities Report. Indianapolis Deaneries. Indianapolis, IN: Catholic Youth Organization, October 1988–October 1989.

Catholic Youth Organization. *25 Years of Memories*. Annual Activities Report. Indianapolis Deaneries. Indianapolis, IN: Catholic Youth Organization, October 1963–October 1964.

Chicago History Museum. "Golden Gloves, Youthful Spirit." http://blog.chicagohistory.org/index.php/2009/05/chicago-boxing.

CYO of Indianapolis Archdiocese. CYO Handbook. Indianapolis, IN: CYO of Indianapolis Archdiocese, 1982.

Dellinger, R.W. "'Play Like a Champion,' CYO Sports Program Encourages Coaches and Players." *Tidings*, February 1, 2008. http://www.catholic.org/printer_friendly.php?id=26694&section=Cathcom.

Encyclopedia of Chicago. "Catholic Youth Organization." http://www.encyclopedia.chicagohistory.org/pages/220.html.

Encyclopedia of Children and Childhood in History and Society. http://www.faqs.org/childhood/Ar-Bo/Boxing.html.

Evans, Brandon A. "Youth and Adults Prepare for World Youth Day." *Criterion*, May 27, 2005.

50th Anniversary of St. Therese Church (Church of the Little Flower) 1925–1975. Indianapolis, IN: produced by Little Flower Parish, 1975.

Hoopedia. "Catholic Youth Organization Boys Tournament (Chicago)." http://hoopedia.nba.com/index.php?title=Catholic_Youth_Organization_Boys_Tournament_%28Chicago%29.

JFK Library. John F. Kennedy Remarks in New York City at the National Convention of the Catholic Youth Organization, November 15, 1963. http://www.jfklibrary.org/Asset-Viewer/Archives/JFKWHA-240-005.aspx.

Poremba, Sue. "The Relationship between Athlete and Coach" Suite 101. http://www.suite101.com/article.cfm/parents_of_athletes/59425.

Science Fair Secrets. "History of Science Fairs." http://www.scienceprojectfair.net/scienceprojectfair03.php.

Shaughnessy, John. "New Bishop Chatard Leader Says Values, Faith Will Guide Him." *Criterion* online, March 2, 2007. http://www.bishopchatard.org/aboutUs/Vision.

Sinatra, Frank. "What Does the CYO Mean to Los Angeles?" League Lineup. http://www.leaguelineup.com/miscinfo.asp?menuid=39&cmenuid=39&url=cyousa&sid=419891818.

Malinowski, Jon, and Christopher Thurber. "A History of Summer Camp." Summer Camp Handbook, 2009. http://www.summercamphandbook.com/161-a-history-of-summer-camp.html.

Time. "The Bishop's 25th." May 11, 1953. http://www.time.com/time/magazine/article/0,9171,935339,00.html.

———. "Defeat in Chicago." December 20, 1954. http://www.time.com/time/magazine/article/0,9171,821045,00.html.

———. "Roman Catholics: No-Nonsense Archbishop." May 20, 1966. http://www.time.com/time/magazine/article/0,9171,835601,00.html?promoid=googlep.

Treat, Roger L. *Bishop Sheil and the CYO*. New York: Julian Messner, Inc., 1951.

Vitek, John, ed. *My Dear Young Friends: Pope John Paul II Speaks to Teens on Life, Love and Courage*. Winona, MN: Saint Mary's Press, 2001.

Wikipedia. "Kickball." http://en.wikipedia.org/wiki/Kickball.

World Youth Day. www.worldyouthday.com.

Wyand, Mary Ann. "Prince of Peace Teenagers Embracing Pro-Life Advocacy." *Criterion*, February 5, 2010.

About the Author

Julie Young is the award-winning author of several local history books, including *A Brief History of Shelby County*, *Eastside Indianapolis: A Brief History*, *Images of America: Historic Irvington* and *A Belief in Providence: A Life of Saint Theodora Guerin*. She is a correspondent for a number of local, regional and national publications, including *Michiana House & Home*, *Glo* magazine, the *Indianapolis Star*, the *Catholic Moment* and *Today's Catholic Teacher*. She lives near Indianapolis with her two sons.